THE INDEX OF
LEADING CULTURAL
INDICATORS

*American Society at the End
of the 20th Century*

Other Books by William J. Bennett

The Death of Outrage

Our Sacred Honor

Body Count

The Children's Book of Virtues

The Moral Compass

The Book of Virtues

The De-Valuing of America

THE INDEX OF LEADING CULTURAL INDICATORS

American Society at the End of the 20th Century

Updated and Expanded

William J. Bennett

Editor of *The Book of Virtues*

Broadway Books
New York

WaterBrook Press
Colorado Springs

BROADWAY

WATERBROOK
PRESS

INDEX OF LEADING CULTURAL INDICATORS. Copyright © 1999 by William J. Bennett. All rights reserved. Printed in the United States of America. No part of this book may be reproduced or transmitted in any form or by any means, electronic or mechanical, including photocopying, recording, or by any information storage and retrieval system, without written permission from the publisher. For information, address Broadway Books, a division of Random House, Inc., 1540 Broadway, New York, NY 10036.

This book is copublished with WaterBrook Press, a division of Random House, Inc., 5446 North Academy Boulevard, Suite 200, Colorado Springs, CO 80918.

Churches, youth groups, and ministries please call 1–800–603–7051, ext. 232, at WaterBrook Press for volume discounts and special sales information.

Broadway Books titles may be purchased for business or promotional use or for special sales. For information, please write to: Special Markets Department, Random House, Inc., 1540 Broadway, New York, NY 10036.

BROADWAY BOOKS and its logo, a letter B bisected on the diagonal, are trademarks of Broadway Books, a division of Random House, Inc.

Visit our website at www.broadwaybooks.com

Library of Congress Cataloging–in–Publication Data
Bennett, William J. (William John), 1943–
    The index of leading cultural indicators : American society at the end of the 20th century / William J. Bennett.
        p. cm.
    Rev. and expanded ed.
    Includes bibliographical references.
    ISBN 0-385-49912-4
    1. Social indicators–United States.   2. United States–Social conditions–1945– Statistics.   I. Title.
    HN60.B46 1999
    306'.0973–dc21

                                                            99–42788
                                                            CIP

FIRST EDITION

Designed by Anne DeLozier

WaterBrook ISBN 1-57856-344-5

99 00 01 02 03 10 9 8 7 6 5 4 3 2 1

CONTENTS

THE INDEX OF LEADING CULTURAL INDICATORS

American Society at the End of the 20th Century

INTRODUCTION

A decade ago the Berlin Wall was reduced to rubble, marking the collapse of the Soviet empire and the culmination of an extraordinary historical epoch. Our "long, twilight struggle" against Soviet communism had ended in a stunning victory for America and the West. But the end of the Cold War also ushered in a period of intense self-examination in this country. With American ideals having prevailed abroad, the dominant question became: *how are we doing at home?*

At that time, despite unparalleled economic prosperity and military supremacy, there was a widespread sense that we were in the midst of a decades-long cultural decline. Was this in fact the case? If so, how serious was it? In which areas had we lost the most ground? Were there *any* areas that had seen improvement?

Much of the discussion of this issue, while thoughtful and instructive, was anecdotal, impressionistic, and speculative. Missing were objective measurements, the cultural equivalents of the Index of Leading Economic Indicators: that is, reliable data, compiled in an easily accessible manner, on the moral, social, and cultural condition of modern American society. Five years ago, in an attempt to respond to the need, I published *The Index of Leading Cultural Indicators*. My conclusion, on the basis of the long-term trends indicated by the data I had collected, was that, yes, we had indeed experienced substantial cultural decline. To be specific, virtually every important indicator not only got worse, it got much worse. I wrote then that unless these exploding social pathologies were reversed, they would lead to the decline—and perhaps even to the fall—of the American republic. The situation was that bad.

This book is an updated, expanded version of the original *Index*; it includes more charts and graphs, more tables, more facts and figures on more subjects than the original. To my knowledge, it is the most comprehensive statistical portrait available of social trends since the 1960s.

The Index of Leading Cultural Indicators: American Society at the End of the 20th Century offers chapters on crime, the family, youth behavior, education, popular culture and religion, and civic participation. It compares America with the rest of the world and, decade by decade, with itself; it ranks the fifty states and the District of Columbia. Each chapter provides an extensive factual presentation, including statistical and numerical breakdowns beginning in 1960 and ending (in most cases) in 1997.

What, briefly, can we learn from this exercise? Since the publication of the last *Index*, there have been many significant, positive developments. The decade of the nineties has seen progress in some key social indicators: reductions in welfare, violent crime, abortion, AIDS, divorce, and suicide; upswings in SAT scores and charitable giving.

A closer look reveals some truly remarkable gains. Since 1994, for example, there has been a 46.5 percent decrease in welfare rolls. The murder rate is at its lowest point since 1967. Alcohol-related traffic fatalities are at their lowest level since the government began keeping such statistics. Since 1993, the reported number of AIDS cases has decreased by more than

50 percent. Near the end of the decade, there are 243,000 fewer abortions per year than at the beginning. There has been a 16–point increase in SAT scores and a 38 percent increase in charitable giving (in inflation–adjusted dollars).

But that is hardly the whole picture. During these same 1990s, we also experienced social regression in several important areas. The percentage of births to unwed mothers—already at the alarmingly high level of 28 percent at the beginning of the decade—is even higher today, at 32.4 percent. America still has the highest divorce rate among Western nations, and the highest incidence of single–parent families of any industrialized nation. Among men and women between their mid–twenties and mid–thirties, living together before marriage is far more common than not. Our rates of sexually transmitted disease far exceed those of every other developed country. In 1998, 5.6 percent of high school seniors reported using marijuana on a daily basis—a 180 percent increase since 1991. In math achievement, American twelfth graders rank nineteenth out of twenty–one nations.

The trends, then, are decidedly mixed, giving rise to opposing interpretations. One camp of observers is quite upbeat, even celebratory; in another camp, occupied mostly by social conservatives, the mood is one of resignation, even despair. In fact, some celebration *is* in order; authentic gains have been achieved. But the worrisome trends are deeply worrisome—afflicting in particular the American family—and we need to think about them afresh.

The first task is to see what we can learn from the decade's successes. Over the last few years, I have amended some of my own prior views about the efficacy of politics and public policy. It turns out that some social pathologies are less resistant to legislative action and political leadership than I once thought. Consider two examples: the extraordinary transformation of New York City, which was once thought to be virtually ungovernable; and the enormous drop in the welfare caseload following the passage of reform legislation. In short, problems that were considered all but intractable have yielded to well-conceived and well-executed reforms.

Can these positive trends be sustained, or even extended to other areas? Certainly there is no ignoring the magnitude of the problem. In two generations, America has undergone dramatic and traumatic social change—the kind that one would normally associate with cataclysmic natural events like famine, revolution, or war. Civilizations stand on precious few pillars, and during the last three and a half decades, many of ours have fractured. Although we have learned to live with the situation, much as one might learn to live with a thorn deeply embedded in the flesh, it is important to remind ourselves periodically just how much ground we have lost.

Since 1960, our population has increased by 48 percent. But since 1960, even *taking into account* recent improvements, we have seen a 467 percent increase in violent crime; a 463 percent increase in the numbers of state and federal prisoners; a 461 percent increase in out-of-wedlock births; more than a 200 percent increase in the percentage of children living in single-parent homes; more than a doubling in the teenage suicide rate; a more than 150 percent increase in the number of Americans receiving welfare payments; an almost tenfold increase in the number of cohabiting couples; a doubling of the divorce rate; and a drop of almost 60 points on SAT scores. Since 1973, there have been more than 35 million abortions, increasing from 744,060 in 1973 to 1,365,700 in 1996.

These seismic social changes have had a profound impact on American politics, to the point that it has changed how politicians campaign and how our elected representatives govern. Issues that were once peripheral to politics are now among the most important of all. The outcome of the 2000 presidential campaign could well depend on which candidate deals with cultural issues in the most responsible, serious-minded, careful, and convincing way. Social and cultural issues—symbolized by moments like the horrific school shooting in Littleton, Colorado—are the ones that most concentrate the American mind these days.

Even during a time of record prosperity, many Americans believe that something has gone wrong at the core.

During the last half of this American century, we have made extraordinary progress in medicine, science, and technology. We have advanced the cause of civil rights at home and human rights abroad. We have achieved unprecedented levels of wealth and affluence. The United States offers unparalleled opportunity and freedom. But we have lost something precious in the process.

The nation we live in today is more violent and vulgar, coarse and cynical, rude and remorseless, deviant and depressed, than the one we once inhabited. A popular culture that is often brutal, gruesome, and enamored with death robs many children of their innocence. People kill other people, and themselves, more easily. Men and women abandon each other, and their children, more readily. Marriage and the American family are weaker, more unstable, less normative.

These are social realities, and they pose an enormous challenge to us; it would be self-delusion, and self-defeating, to pretend otherwise. But surely the successes of the nineties do give us something upon which to build. Above all, they remind us that we do not have to sit passively by while our culture breaks apart. To those who believe our decline is inevitable because social trends are irreversible, our answer should be: no, it need not be so, and we will not allow it to happen.

Restoring a civilization's social and moral order—making it more humane, civil, responsible, and just—is no simple task. But America remains what it has always been: an exceptional nation. Our capacity for self-renewal is rare, and real. We have relied on it in the past. For reasons you are about to see, we must call on it again.

CHAPTER ONE

Crime

TOTAL CRIMES

- **Between 1990 and 1997, the total crime rate* fell 15.4 percent. But between 1960 and 1997, the total crime rate rose more than 160 percent.**

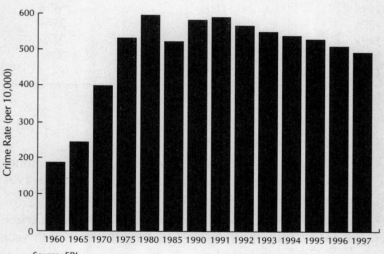

Total Crime Rate

Source: FBI

*Total crimes are defined by the FBI as the violent crimes of murder, rape, robbery, and assault, and the property crimes of burglary, larceny–theft, motor vehicle theft, and arson. For a discussion of how crimes are counted, please see the "Note to the Reader" in the back of the book.

Total Crime

Year	Total Crimes	Total Crime Rate (per 10,000)
1960	3,384,200	188.7
1965	4,739,400	244.9
1970	8,098,000	398.5
1975	11,292,400	529.9
1980	13,408,300	595.0
1985	12,431,400	520.7
1990	14,475,600	582.0
1991	14,872,900	589.8
1992	14,438,200	566.0
1993	14,144,800	548.4
1994	13,989,500	537.4
1995	13,862,700	527.6
1996	13,493,900	508.7
1997	13,175,070	492.3

Source: FBI

Factual Overview: Total Crime

- In 1997, there were slightly more than 13 million crimes reported in the United States. This is down from the 1991 peak, in which there were almost 15 million crimes.[1]

- According to preliminary numbers from 1998, total crime was down 7 percent from 1997, making it the seventh year in a row crime declined.[2]

- The decline from 1992 to 1998 is the longest consecutive decline in crime since the 1950s.[3]

- Both males and females, whites and blacks, and people of all income levels experienced declines in the criminal victimization rate between 1993 and 1997.[4]

- In 1997, households with annual incomes of below $7,500 were burglarized at a rate approximately double that of households with incomes above $25,000 per year.[5]

- In 1997, the most common type of criminal offense was larceny–theft (58.6 percent), followed by burglary (18.7 per-cent) and motor vehicle theft (10.3 percent). Murder accounted for 0.1 percent and forcible rape for 0.7 percent.[6]

- In the early 1990s, the violent crimes committed in this country each year cost victims and society more than $400 billion.[7]

- Estimates of the average number of crimes committed by prisoners in the year prior to their incarceration range from twelve to twenty–one.[8]

- The overall arrest rate in the United States in 1997 was 5,752.1 for every 100,000 inhabitants.[9] Two–thirds of arrestees were white and 30 percent were black.*[10]

- Persons aged 16 to 39 make up 36 percent of the population and account for almost three–quarters of all arrests.[11]

The States: Crime Rates

- In 1997, the United States averaged 492.3 crimes per 10,000 residents. The District of Columbia† had the highest crime rate and West Virginia had the lowest crime rate.[12]

---

* The reason Hispanics do not appear in FBI statistics is that when the FBI col-lects data on the race of offenders and victims, it does not count Hispanics as a separate category. Rather, it defines Hispanics as an ethnicity and groups Hispanics under the appropriate racial category (sometimes grouped as blacks, and other times as whites). The Bureau of Justice Statistics, on the other hand, does count Hispanics as a separate category in some cases.

† In this book, the District of Columbia is included in state–by–state compar-isons. For more information, see the "Note to the Reader" in the back of the book.

Crime Rates by State, 1997

State	Total Crimes	Total Crime Rate (per 10,000)
District of Columbia	52,049	983.9
Florida	1,065,609	727.2
Arizona	327,734	719.5
New Mexico	119,483	690.7
Louisiana	280,671	644.9
Oregon	203,328	627.0
South Carolina	230,637	613.4
Nevada	101,702	606.5
Hawaii	71,492	602.3
Utah	123,447	599.6
Washington	332,466	592.6
Georgia	433,563	579.2
Maryland	287,969	565.3
Tennessee	295,873	551.2
Oklahoma	182,258	549.5
North Carolina	407,743	549.2
Texas	1,065,357	548.1
Alaska	32,110	527.3
Illinois	611,589	514.1
Delaware	37,612	513.8
United States	**13,175,070**	**492.3**
Michigan	480,579	491.7
Alabama	211,188	489.0
California	1,569,949	486.5
Missouri	260,081	481.5
Arkansas	119,052	471.9
Colorado	181,041	465.0
Mississippi	126,452	463.0
Kansas	118,422	456.4
Ohio	505,005	451.5

(continued next page)

State	Total Crimes	Total Crime Rate (per 10,000)
Indiana	261,902	446.6
Minnesota	206,833	441.4
Montana	38,753	440.9
Nebraska	70,982	428.4
Wyoming	20,068	418.1
New Jersey	326,711	405.7
Connecticut	130,286	398.4
Idaho	47,495	392.5
New York	709,328	391.1
Virginia	261,022	387.6
Iowa	108,827	381.6
Wisconsin	190,133	367.8
Massachusetts	224,848	367.5
Rhode Island	36,069	365.4
Pennsylvania	412,463	343.2
South Dakota	23,948	324.5
Maine	38,896	313.2
Kentucky	122,205	312.7
Vermont	16,658	282.8
North Dakota	17,380	271.1
New Hampshire	30,963	264.0
West Virginia	44,839	246.9

Factual Overview: Police Deployment and Personal Security

- In 1996, there were about 738,000 full-time, sworn law-enforcement officers in the United States.[13]

- In 1965, there were 19 full-time police officers for every 10,000 citizens. Currently, there are 25 for every 10,000 citizens.[14] In 1996, the state with the highest rate of full-time law-enforcement officers was the District of Columbia, with

72 for every 10,000 residents. West Virginia was the lowest with 16 per 10,000 residents.[15]

- Between 1980 and 1996, state expenditures (in dollars per capita) on police protection have increased 170 percent. State expenditures per capita on corrections (costs of jails, prisons, probation, parole, etc.) have increased 415 percent.[16]

- College campuses average 30 full-time police officers.[17]

- In 1996, New York City's police department had the most full-time employees (36,813), followed by Chicago's (13,237).[18]

- In 1998, Americans spent $15.23 billion on personal-security systems.[19]

VIOLENT CRIMES

- *Between 1990 and 1997, the violent crime* rate decreased 17 percent. Between 1960 and 1997, the rate increased 280 percent.*

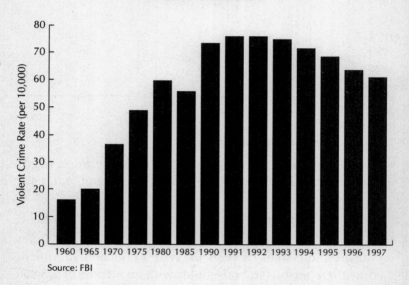

Violent Crime Rate

Source: FBI

---

* Violent crimes are defined by the FBI as murder, rape, robbery, and aggravated assault.

Violent Crimes

Year	Violent Crimes	Violent Crime Rate (per 10,000)
1960	288,460	16.1
1965	387,390	20.0
1970	738,820	36.4
1975	1,039,710	48.8
1980	1,344,520	59.7
1985	1,328,800	55.7
1990	1,820,130	73.2
1991	1,911,770	75.8
1992	1,932,270	75.8
1993	1,926,020	74.7
1994	1,857,670	71.4
1995	1,798,790	68.5
1996	1,688,540	63.7
1997	1,634,773	61.1

Source: FBI

Factual Overview: Violent Crime

- In 1997, there were 1,634,773 reported violent crimes: 18,209 murders, 96,122 rapes, 497,950 robberies, and 1,022,492 assaults.[20]

- The violent crime rate in 1997 was the lowest since 1987.[21]

- Persons in households with an income of under $7,500 per year are more than twice as likely to be victims of violent crime than persons in households with an income of $75,000 or more.[22]

- In 1997, almost 85 percent of persons arrested for violent crimes were males.[23]

- Whites comprise approximately 82 percent of the population and account for 54.6 percent of all violent offender arrests.[24]

- Blacks comprise approximately 13 percent of the population and account for 43.2 percent of all violent offender arrests.[25]
- While decreasing crime rates have affected most demographic segments of the population, violent victimization rates for persons aged 50 and older are no lower than they were in 1993.[26]
- In 1997, persons aged 12 to 19 were about twice as likely as persons aged 25 to 34—and about three times as likely as persons aged 35 to 49—to be victims of violent crimes. Persons aged 12 to 19 had a violent-crime victimization rate about twenty times that of persons aged 65 or older.[27]
- Surveys of violent-crime victimization have found that 12.6 married women per 1,000 are victims of violent crime, while 43.9 never-married women per 1,000 and 66.5 divorced or separated women per 1,000 are victims of violent crime.[28]

Factual Overview: Murder

- There were 18,209 murders in 1997.[29]
- According to preliminary FBI statistics, the number of murders decreased 8 percent between 1997 and 1998.[30]
- The murder rate decreased 28 percent between 1993 and 1997. The murder rate (6.8 murders for every 100,000 inhabitants) is at its lowest since 1967.[31]
- There are fewer than 20,000 murders a year in America and about 30,000 suicides.[32]
- In New York City, the number of murders went from 2,245 in 1990 to 633 in 1998—a decrease of more than 70 percent.[33]
- In 1998, Chicago had more murders (694) than New York City (633) even though New York's population is almost three times as large.[34]
- Nearly half of all murder victims know their assailants.[35]

- Of the ten U.S. cities with the most homicides in 1990, each has seen a substantial reduction in the homicide rate— except Baltimore.[36]

Ten Major U.S. Cities and the Change in Homicide Rates, 1990–97

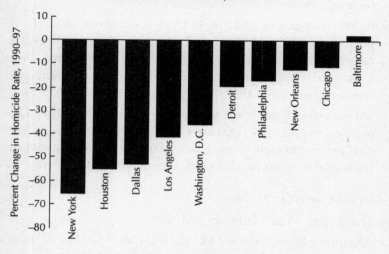

Ten Major U.S. Cities and the Change in Homicide Rates, 1990–97

City	Percent Change
New York	−65.7
Houston	−55.3
Dallas	−53.2
Los Angeles	−41.4
Washington, D.C.	−36.2
Detroit	−19.4
Philadelphia	−16.9
New Orleans	−12.2
Chicago	−11.0
Baltimore	+2.2

- The homicide offending rate for males (14.1 per 100,000) is almost ten times that for females (1.5 per 100,000).[37]

- Almost 70 percent of all homicides involve male victims and male perpetrators.[38]

- Blacks comprise about 13 percent of the population and account for almost half of the murder victims and more than half of all murderers whose race was known.[39]

- Between 1976 and 1997, 85 percent of white murder victims were killed by whites, and 94 percent of black murder victims were killed by blacks.[40]

- The rate of black males aged 18 to 24 who commit murder is almost nine times that of white males in the same age group. At the same time, the rate of black males in that age group who are victims of homicide is more than nine times that of white males.[41]

- While black males aged 14 to 24 comprise just over 1 percent of the population, they account for almost 30 percent of all homicide offenders and just under 17 percent of all homicide victims.[42]

Factual Overview: Guns

- Estimates are that between 75 and 86 million Americans own between 200 and 240 million guns. About a third of all guns owned by Americans are handguns.[43]

- Firearms were used in almost 70 percent of murders in 1997— and of the roughly 10,000 homicides involving firearms, handguns were used in more than three-quarters of them.[44]

- Of the 31,284 suicides in 1995, 12 percent were committed with handguns and 47 percent with other firearms.[45]

- The death rate for Americans involving firearms in 1995 was 13.9 per 100,000 citizens. The death rate involving firearms for whites was less than half of that for blacks.[46]

- While 18-to-20-year-olds make up about 4 percent of the population, they commit almost one-quarter of all gun-related homicides.[47]

- The number of murders involving firearms decreased 36 percent between 1993 and 1997.[48]

- Less than 30 percent of all violent crimes involve the use of firearms.[49]

- In 1995, 12.7 percent of students knew someone who brought a gun to school.[50]

- In 1996, 40 percent of Americans reported having a firearm in their home. Of these, 62 percent reported having a shotgun, 58 percent a rifle, and 56 percent a pistol.[51]

- Between 1976 and 1996, the percentage of Americans reporting a gun in their household decreased 15 percent.[52]

- Of guns obtained by violent criminals, 93 percent are not obtained through the lawful purchase and sale transactions that are the object of most gun-control legislation.[53]

- Armed citizens defend their lives or property with firearms against criminals approximately 1 million times a year. In 98 percent of these instances, the citizen brandishes the weapon or fires a warning shot. Only in 2 percent of the cases do citizens actually shoot their assailants. In defending themselves with their firearms, armed citizens kill 2,000 to 3,000 criminals each year—three times the number killed by police.[54]

JUVENILE VIOLENT CRIME

- **Between 1990 and 1996, the juvenile violent crime arrest rate increased 11 percent. Between 1965 and 1996, the rate increased 215 percent.[55]**

Juvenile Violent Crime Arrest Rate

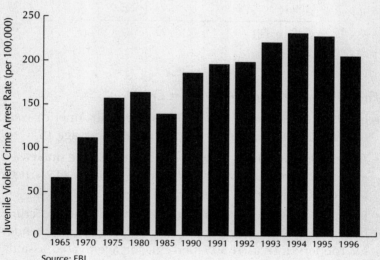

Source: FBI

Juvenile Violent Crime Arrest Rate

Year	Rate (per 100,000)
1965	65.1
1970	110.6
1975	155.7
1980	162.5
1985	137.9
1990	184.8
1991	195.0
1992	197.6
1993	220.5
1994	231.3
1995	227.9
1996	205.0

Source: FBI

Factual Overview: Juvenile Violent Crime

- In 1997, 19 percent of all persons arrested in America were under the age of 18, and 6 percent were under age 15.[56]

- The female juvenile violent crime arrest rate increased almost 42 percent between 1990 and 1996, from 44.9 arrests per 100,000 female juveniles to 63.7 arrests.[57]

- Between 1988 and 1997, arrests for juvenile violent crime increased 48.9 percent. The number of arrests of juveniles for robbery increased 55.7 percent; for aggravated assault, 51.4 percent; for arson, 21.9 percent; and for murder, 10.6 percent. The number of arrests for motor vehicle thefts, however, decreased 17 percent.[58]

Juvenile Violent Crime Arrests, Selected Offenses 1988 and 1997

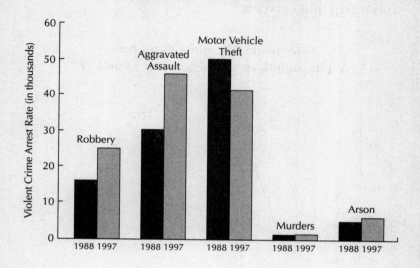

Juvenile Violent Crime Arrests, Selected Offenses 1988 and 1997

Crime	1988	1997
Robbery	16,094	25,065
Aggravated assault	30,428	46,072
Motor vehicle theft	50,239	41,684
Murders	1,397	1,545
Arson	5,028	6,127

• Homicide rates for juvenile males between the ages of 14
and 17 tripled between 1977 and 1993. Since then, rates have
decreased by 45 percent.[59]

Homicide Offending Rates for
White and Black Males Between 14 and 17

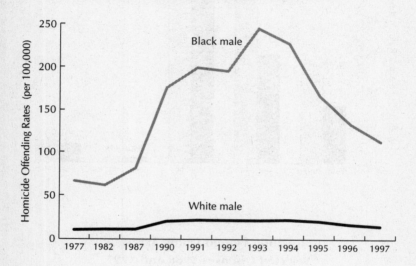

Homicide Offending Rates (per 100,000) for White and Black Males Between 14 and 17

Year	Total	White Male	Black Male
1977	10.0	10.6	66.6
1982	10.4	11.3	61.6
1987	12.3	11.4	81.7
1990	23.7	20.6	175.3
1991	26.6	21.9	199.1
1992	26.3	21.8	195.2

(continued next page)

Year	Total	White Male	Black Male
1993	30.2	21.8	244.1
1994	29.3	22.4	226.7
1995	23.6	20.8	165.8
1996	19.6	17.2	133.5
1997	16.5	15.0	112.3

- In 1997, there were more than 2,000 burglaries by children under 10 and almost 7,000 episodes of larceny–theft. For children between the ages of 10 and 12, there were more than 4,000 incidents of aggravated assault and more than 41,000 thefts.[60]

- While the overall juvenile homicide arrest rate has fallen since 1990, the juvenile homicide arrest rate in rural areas has increased by 56.6 percent.[61]

- In 1997, 8.5 percent of high school students reported carrying a weapon (e.g., a gun, knife, or club) on school property, and 7.4 percent were threatened or injured with a weapon on school property.[62]

- About 6 percent of male juveniles are arrested five or more times before age 18, accounting for more than half of crimes, and about two–thirds of the violent crimes, committed by the entire juvenile male population.[63]

IMPRISONMENT

- *Between 1990 and 1997, the rate of sentenced prisoners in the United States increased 50 percent. Between 1960 and 1997, the rate increased 280 percent.*

Rate of Sentenced Prisoners in State and Federal Institutions

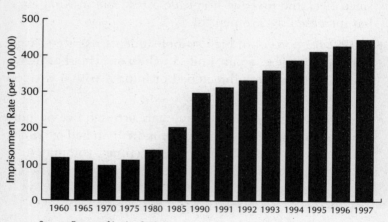

Source: Bureau of Justice Statistics

Sentenced Prisoners in State and Federal Institutions

Year	Prisoners (total number)	Rate (per 100,000 residents)
1960	212,953	117
1965	210,895	108
1970	196,429	96
1975	240,593	111
1980	315,974	139
1985	480,568	202
1990	739,980	297
1991	789,610	313
1992	846,277	332
1993	932,074	359
1994	1,016,691	389
1995	1,085,363	411
1996	1,138,984	427
1997	1,197,590	445

Source: Bureau of Justice Statistics

Factual Overview: Imprisonment

• In 1998, there were more than 1.8 million persons in federal and state prisons *and* local jails.[65]

• About 45 percent of the growth in prison populations between 1997 and 1998 occurred in four states—Texas (6,700), California (5,732), Louisiana (2,525), and Ohio (2,041)—and the federal prison system (8,748).[66]

• An estimated one out of every twenty people will serve time in prison during their lifetime. Men are eight times as likely as women to serve time in prison.[67]

• An estimated 28.5 percent of black men, 16 percent of Hispanic men, and 4 percent of white men can be expected to serve a state or federal prison term.[68]

- While the national population increased 15 percent between 1980 and 1994, the nation's prison population increased by 213 percent, and the probation population increased by exactly the same percentage.[69]

- Less than one-third of the 5.69 million adults under correctional supervision in 1997 were in jail or prison—57 percent of them were on probation and 12 percent were on parole.[70]

- Between 1990 and 1997, violent offenders accounted for 50 percent of the increase in the nation's prison population; drug offenders accounted for 25 percent of the increase.[71]

- During the 1960s, while crime rates soared, there was a decline in the number of prisoners—state and federal—from about 213,000 in 1960 to about 196,400 in 1970.[72]

- In 1995, there were 1,500 prisons—an increase of 213 since 1990.[73]

- The five largest local jail jurisdictions, based on the number of inmates held:[74]

  Los Angeles County, CA: 21,268
  New York City, NY: 17,680
  Cook County, IL: 9,321
  Harris County, TX: 7,587
  Dade County, FL: 7,036

The States: Highest and Lowest Incarceration Rates

- Louisiana had the highest incarceration rate of any state in 1998, while Minnesota had the lowest rate.[75]

**Incarceration Rates
(per 100,000 residents)**

Highest	Lowest
Louisiana: 709	Minnesota: 117
Texas: 700	Maine: 121
Oklahoma: 629	North Dakota: 126
Mississippi: 547	Vermont: 170
South Carolina: 543	New Hampshire: 183

PUNISHMENT

- *Between 1990 and 1996, the expected time in prison* for serious crimes increased 20.6 percent. But between 1960 and 1996, the rate decreased 27 percent.*[76]

Expected Prison Time for Serious Crimes

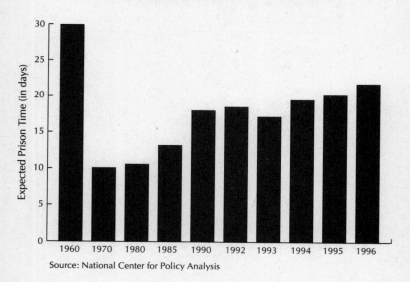

Source: National Center for Policy Analysis

* The National Center for Policy Analysis calculates expected prison time by multiplying four probabilities (of being arrested, of being prosecuted, of being convicted if prosecuted, and of going to prison if convicted) and then multiplying the product by the median time served for an offense. Serious crimes are defined as murder, rape, robbery, assault, and burglary.

Expected Prison Time for Serious Crimes

Year	Expected Prison Time (in days)
1960	29.9
1970	10.1
1980	10.6
1985	13.2
1990	18.0
1992	18.5
1993	17.2
1994	19.5
1995	20.2
1996	21.7

Source: National Center for Policy Analysis

Factual Overview: Punishment

- Since 1960, the expected prison time for murder has increased, while that for rape, robbery, aggravated assault, and burglary has decreased. During the 1980s and the 1990s, however, the expected prison time for every serious offense increased.[77]

Expected Prison Times for Various Offenses

Year	Murder (in years)	Rape (in days)	Robbery (in days)	Aggravated Assault (in days)	Burglary (in days)
1960	1.8	154	93	19	14
1970	1.1	67	30	8	3
1980	1.2	42	34	7	4
1990	2.5	111	45	12	7
1996	3.1	119	52	13	8

• The mean sentence for a violent offender released in 1996 was eighty-five months, of which about forty-five months were served.[78]

Mean Sentence Length vs. Time Served, 1996

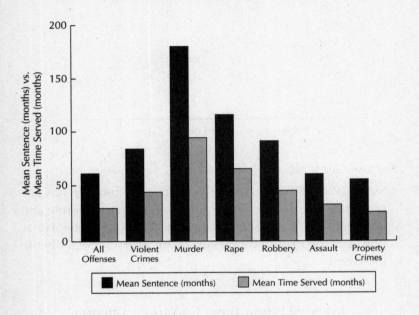

Mean Sentence Length vs. Time Served, 1996

Crime	Mean Sentence (months)	Mean Time Served (months)
All offenses	62	30
All violent crimes	85	45
Murder	180	95
Rape	116	66

(continued next page)

Crime	Mean Sentence (months)	Mean Time Served (months)
Robbery	92	46
Assault	61	33
Property crimes	56	26

- Between 1993 and 1996, the odds of going to prison for murder increased 53 percent, and the murder rate decreased 30 percent. As the odds of going to prison for rape, robbery, aggravated assault, and burglary have increased, the rates of these crimes have decreased.[79]

- Truth-in-sentencing laws increased the average time served by released prisoners convicted of a violent crime up from forty-three months in 1993 to forty-nine months in 1997. For all types of prisoners, the average time served increased from twenty-two months in 1990 to twenty-five months in 1996.[80]

- Offenders released from prison for rape in 1996 served on average sixty-six months (52.6 percent of their sentence), up from sixty-two months (45.5 percent of their sentence) for those released from prison in 1990.[81]

- On average, federal inmates serve six and a half years of a ten-and-a-half-year sentence, and state inmates serve five and a half years of a sentence of twelve and a half years.[82]

- Law-enforcement agencies made approximately 2.7 million arrests in 1997.[83]

DRUG USE

- *Between 1992 and 1997, there was a 10 percent increase in the percentage of Americans reporting the use of any illegal drug within the past thirty days. But between 1979 and 1997, we have seen a 55 percent decrease in illegal drug use.*[84]

Percent of Americans Who Have Used Any Illegal Drug in the Past Month

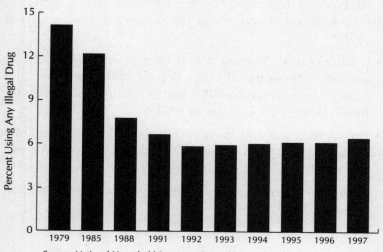

Source: National Household Survey on Drug Abuse

Percent of Americans Who Have Used
Any Illegal Drug in the Past Month

Year	Any Illegal Drug	Marijuana	Cocaine
1979	14.1	13.2	2.6
1982	NA	11.5	2.4
1985	12.1	9.7	3.0
1988	7.7	6.2	1.6
1991	6.6	5.1	1.0
1992	5.8	4.7	0.7
1993	5.9	4.6	0.7
1994	6.0	4.8	0.7
1995	6.1	4.7	0.7
1996	6.1	4.7	0.8
1997	6.4	5.1	0.7

Source: National Household Survey on Drug Abuse

Factual Overview: Illegal Drugs

- Between 1979 and 1997, there was a more than 60 percent decrease in the use of marijuana.[85]

- Between 1985 and 1997, there was a 77 percent decrease in the use of cocaine.[86]

- While the population has increased by 20 percent since 1979, the number of current drug users (that is, people who reported using drugs in the past thirty days) is about 55 percent of what it was in 1979.[87]

- Almost half of all heroin users currently in treatment have previously been in treatment three or more times.[88]

- Seventy-four million living Americans have tried an illegal drug at least once in their lifetime.[89]

- In 1997, 57 percent of state prisoners reported having used drugs in the month before their offense, up from 50 percent in 1991. For federal prisoners, the number rose from 32 percent in 1991 to 45 percent in 1997.[90]

- On the federal level, in 1997, 85.8 percent of drug offenders were imprisoned for trafficking, versus 5.3 percent for possession. On the state level, 70.1 percent were imprisoned for trafficking and 27.1 percent for possession.[91]

- Nearly three-quarters of federal prisoners used illegal drugs in the past.[92]

- Americans spend more than $57 billion annually on illegal drugs, $38 billion of which is spent on cocaine, $9.6 billion on heroin, $7 billion on marijuana, and $2.7 billion on other drugs.[93]

- The economic cost of drug abuse totals more than $100 billion per year. It increased 82 percent between 1985 and 1995.[94]

- Between 1990 and 1996, the population increased 6.3 percent, and murders related to drugs declined 40 percent. Drug-induced deaths, however, increased 64 percent between 1990 and 1995, while the population increased 5.3 percent.[95]

- Drug-related arrests increased 38 percent between 1990 and 1996.[96]

- Between 1990 and 1995, there was a 47 percent increase in the number of emergency room mentions for drug-related episodes.[97]

Drug–Related Emergency Room Cases

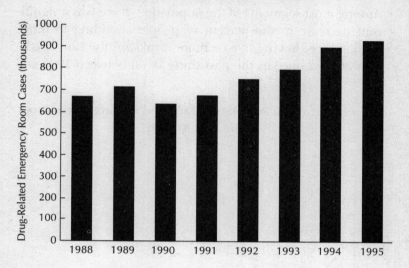

Drug–Related Emergency Room Cases

Year	Total	Cocaine	Heroin
1988	668,153	101,578	38,063
1989	713,392	110,013	41,656
1990	635,460	80,355	33,884
1991	674,861	101,189	35,898
1992	751,731	119,843	48,003
1993	796,762	123,423	63,232
1994	900,317	142,878	64,013
1995	931,550	142,494	76,023

Factual Overview: Alcohol Abuse

• Among most segments of the population, there was a significant decrease in the percent of people admitting to binge drinking (i.e., having five or more drinks on the same occasion at least once in the past thirty days) between 1985 and 1997.[98]

Percentage of the Population Engaged in Binge Drinking in the Past Month

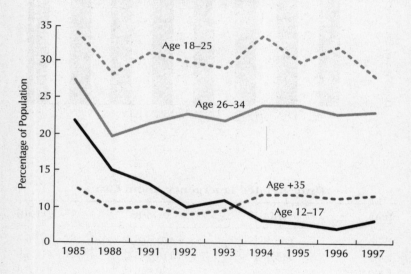

Percentage of the Population Engaged in Binge Drinking in the Past Month

Age	1985	1988	1991	1992	1993	1994	1995	1996	1997
12–17	21.9	15.1	13.2	10.0	11.0	8.3	7.9	7.2	8.3
18–25	34.4	28.2	31.2	29.9	29.1	33.6	29.9	32.0	28.0
26–34	27.5	19.7	21.5	22.8	21.9	24.0	24.0	22.8	23.1
35+	12.9	9.7	10.1	9.0	9.6	11.8	11.8	11.3	11.7

- Although annual per capita consumption of alcohol decreased 10 percent between 1990 and 1995, the average American still drinks 35.9 gallons of alcohol per year.[99]

Factual Overview: Alcohol and Crime

- Only one in five alcohol–related violent incidents involves a weapon. Firearms were involved in about one in twenty-five violent incidents in which alcohol was considered to be a factor.[100]

- In 1998, according to preliminary estimates, there were 15,936 alcohol–related traffic fatalities—the lowest level since 1975, when the government began keeping the statistics.[101]

- Arrests for drunken driving fell from 1.8 million in 1986 to about 1.5 million in 1997—a decrease of 18 percent in a period when the number of licensed drivers increased 15 percent.[102]

- In 1996, there were more than 2.7 million alcohol–related arrests (DUI, liquor law violations, drunkenness, disorderly conduct, and vagrancy).[103]

- Nearly four in ten violent victimizations involve use of alcohol, and about four in ten offenders—regardless of whether they are on probation, in local jail, or in state prison—self-report that they were using alcohol at the time of the offense.[104]

NOTES

[1] U.S. Department of Justice, Federal Bureau of Investigation, *Crime in the United States 1997* (Washington, DC: GPO, 1998).

[2] U.S. Department of Justice, Federal Bureau of Investigation, *UCR Preliminary Crime Statistics 1998.*

[3] Fox Butterfield, "Crime Fell 7 Percent in '98, Continuing a 7–Year Trend," *New York Times,* May 17, 1999.

[4] U.S. Department of Justice, Bureau of Justice Statistics, "Criminal Victimization 1997."

[5] Ibid.

[6] U.S. Department of Justice, Federal Bureau of Investigation, *Crime in the United States 1997* (Washington, DC: GPO, 1998).

[7] Mark A. Cohen et al., *Crime in the United States: Victim Costs and Consequences* (Washington, DC: National Institute of Justice, 1995).

[8] Thomas B. Marvell and Carlisle B. Moody, "Prison Population Growth and Crime Reduction," *Journal of Quantitative Criminology*, 1994; Anne Morrison Piehl and John J. DiIulio, Jr., "Does Prison Pay? Revisited," *Brookings Review*, Winter 1995; Steven D. Levitt, "The Effects of Prison Population Size on Crime Rates," *Quarterly Journal of Economics*, 1996; Anne Morrison Piehl et al., "Right–Sizing Justice: Profiles of Prisoners in Three States" (New York: Center for Civic Innovation, Manhattan Institute, June 1999).

[9] U.S. Department of Justice, Federal Bureau of Investigation, *Crime in the United States 1997* (Washington, DC: GPO, 1998).

[10] U.S. Department of Justice, Federal Bureau of Investigation, *Crime in the United States 1997* (Washington, DC: GPO, 1998).

[11] U.S. Department of Justice, Bureau of Justice Statistics, *Sourcebook of Criminal Justice Statistics 1997* (Washington, DC: GPO, 1998).

[12] U.S. Department of Justice, Federal Bureau of Investigation, *Crime in the United States 1997* (Washington, DC: GPO, 1998).

[13] U.S. Department of Justice, Bureau of Justice Statistics, "Law Enforcement Statistics," *http://www.ojp.usdoj.gov/bjs/lawenf.htm*.

[14] U.S. Department of Justice, Federal Bureau of Investigation, *Crime in the United States 1997* (Washington, DC: GPO, 1998), and U.S. Department of Justice, Federal Bureau of Investigation, *Crime in the United States 1965* (Washington, DC: GPO, 1966).

[15] U.S. Department of Justice, Bureau of Justice Statistics, *Sourcebook of Criminal Justice Statistics 1997* (Washington, DC: GPO, 1998).

[16] U.S. Department of Commerce, Bureau of the Census, *Statistical Abstract of the United States 1998* (Washington, DC: GPO, 1998).

[17] U.S. Department of Justice, Bureau of Justice Statistics, *Sourcebook of Criminal Justice Statistics 1997* (Washington, DC: GPO, 1998).

[18] Ibid.

[19] Security Distribution and Marketing Magazine, 1999 Industry Forecast Study, adjusted for inflation.

[20] U.S. Department of Justice, Federal Bureau of Investigation, *Crime in the United States 1997* (Washington, DC: GPO, 1998).

[21] Ibid.

[22] U.S. Department of Justice, Bureau of Justice Statistics, "Criminal Victimization 1997."

[23] U.S. Department of Justice, Federal Bureau of Investigation, *Crime in the United States 1997* (Washington, DC: GPO, 1998).

[24] U.S. Department of Justice, Bureau of Justice Statistics, *Sourcebook of Criminal Justice Statistics 1997* (Washington, DC: GPO, 1998).

[25] Ibid.

[26] U.S. Department of Justice, Bureau of Justice Statistics, "Criminal Victimization 1997."

[27] Ibid.

[28] David Popenoe, *Life Without Father* (New York: The Free Press, 1996).

[29] U.S. Department of Justice, Federal Bureau of Investigation, *Crime in the United States 1997* (Washington, DC: GPO, 1998).

[30] U.S. Department of Justice, Federal Bureau of Investigation, *UCR Preliminary Crime Statistics 1998.*

[31] U.S. Department of Justice, Federal Bureau of Investigation, *Crime in the United States 1997* (Washington, DC: GPO, 1998).

[32] U.S. Department of Health and Human Services, National Center for Health Statistics, "National Vital Statistics Report," Vol. 47, No. 9.

[33] New York Division of Criminal Justice Services, "Reported Crimes," and U.S. Department of Justice, Federal Bureau of Investigation, *UCR Preliminary Crime Statistics 1998.*

[34] U.S. Department of Justice, Federal Bureau of Investigation, *UCR Preliminary Crime Statistics 1998.*

[35] U.S. Department of Justice, Federal Bureau of Investigation, *Crime in the United States 1997* (Washington, DC: GPO, 1998).

[36] *USA Today*, "Baltimore Homicide Rate Up," March 19, 1999.

[37] U.S. Department of Justice, Bureau of Justice Statistics, "Homicide Trends in the United States," December 11, 1998.

[38] Ibid.

[39] U.S. Department of Justice, Federal Bureau of Investigation, *Crime in the United States 1997* (Washington, DC: GPO, 1998).

[40] U.S. Department of Justice, Bureau of Justice Statistics, "Homicide Trends in the United States," December 11, 1998.

[41] Ibid.

[42] Ibid.

[43] John R. Lott, *More Crime, Less Guns* (Chicago: Chicago UP, 1998).

[44] U.S. Department of Justice, Federal Bureau of Investigation, *Crime in the United States 1997* (Washington, DC: GPO, 1998).

[45] U.S. Department of Commerce, Bureau of the Census, *Statistical Abstract of the United States 1998* (Washington, DC: GPO, 1998).

[46] Ibid.

[47] Terry M. Neal, "Quarter of Gun Deaths Committed by Youths 18 to 20," *Washington Post*, June 14, 1999.

[48] U.S. Department of Justice, Federal Bureau of Investigation, *Crime in the United States 1997* (Washington, DC: GPO, 1998).

[49] U.S. Department of Justice, Bureau of Justice Statistics, *Sourcebook of Criminal Justice Statistics 1997* (Washington, DC: GPO, 1998).

[50] Ibid.

[51] Ibid.

[52] Ibid.

[53] U.S. Department of Justice and Bureau of Alcohol, Tobacco, and Firearms, cited in Jeffrey Snyder, "A Nation of Cowards," *Public Interest*, Fall 1993.

[54] Gary Kleck, Florida State University, cited in *ibid.*

[55] U.S. Department of Justice, Federal Bureau of Investigation, "Age-Specific Arrest Rates for Selected Offenses 1965–1992," and unpublished data for *Crime in the United States 1997* (Washington, DC: GPO, 1998).

[56] U.S. Department of Justice, Federal Bureau of Investigation, *Crime in the United States 1997* (Washington, DC: GPO, 1998).

[57] Ibid.

[58] U.S. Department of Justice, Federal Bureau of Investigation, *Crime in the United States 1997* (Washington, DC: GPO, 1998).

[59] U.S. Department of Justice, Bureau of Justice Statistics, "Homicide Trends in the United States," December 11, 1998.

[60] U.S. Department of Justice, Federal Bureau of Investigation, *Crime in the United States 1997* (Washington, DC: GPO, 1998).

[61] Gary Fields and Paul Overberg, "Juvenile Homicide Arrest Rate on Rise in Rural USA," *USA Today*, March 26, 1998.

[62] U.S. Department of Education, National Center for Education Statistics, *Digest of Education Statistics 1998* (Washington, DC: GPO, 1999).

[63] Marvin E. Wolfgang et al., *Delinquency in a Birth Cohort* (Chicago: Chicago UP, 1972), and *From Boy to Man, From Delinquency to Crime* (Chicago: Chicago UP, 1987).

[64] U.S. Department of Justice, Bureau of Justice Statistics, *Sourcebook of Criminal Justice Statistics 1997* (Washington, DC: GPO, 1998).

[65] U.S. Department of Justice, Bureau of Justice Statistics, "Prison and Jail Inmates at Midyear 1998."

[66] Ibid.

[67] U.S. Department of Justice, Bureau of Justice Statistics, "Criminal Offenders Statistics," http://www.ojp.usdoj.gov/bjs/crimoff.htm.

[68] U.S. Department of Justice, Bureau of Justice Statistics, "Lifetime Likelihood of Going to State or Federal Prison," March 6, 1997.

[69] John J. DiIulio, Jr., "Against Mandatory Minimums," *National Review*, May 17, 1999.

[70] U.S. Department of Justice, Bureau of Justice Statistics, *Sourcebook of Criminal Justice Statistics 1997* (Washington, DC: GPO, 1998).

[71] John J. DiIulio, Jr., "Against Mandatory Minimums," *National Review*, May 17, 1999.

[72] James Q. Wilson, *Thinking about Crime* (New York: Basic Books, 1975).

[73] U.S. Department of Justice, Bureau of Justice Statistics, *Sourcebook of Criminal Justice Statistics 1997* (Washington, DC: GPO, 1998).

[74] U.S. Department of Justice, Bureau of Justice Statistics, "Prison and Jail Inmates at Midyear 1998."

[75] Ibid.

[76] Morgan O. Reynolds, "Crime and Punishment in America: 1998" (Dallas: National Center for Policy Analysis, 1999).

[77] Ibid.

[78] U.S. Department of Justice, Bureau of Justice Statistics, "Truth in Sentencing in State Prisons," January 1999.

[79] Morgan O. Reynolds, "Crime and Punishment in America: 1998" (Dallas: National Center for Policy Analysis, 1999).

[80] John J. DiIulio, Jr., "Against Mandatory Minimums," *National Review*, May 17, 1999.

[81] U.S. Department of Justice, Bureau of Justice Statistics, "Truth in Sentencing in State Prisons," January 1999.

[82] U.S. Department of Justice, Bureau of Justice Statistics, "Criminal Offenders Statistics," http://www.ojp.usdoj.gov/bjs/crimoff.htm.

[83] U.S. Department of Justice, Federal Bureau of Investigation, *Crime in the United States 1997* (Washington, DC: GPO, 1998).

[84] U.S. Department of Health and Human Services, Substance Abuse and Mental Health Statistics, "1997 National Household Survey on Drug Abuse."

[85] Ibid.

[86] Ibid.

[87] Ibid.

[88] Office of National Drug Control Policy, "Data Snapshot: Drug Abuse in America, 1998."

[89] Ibid.

[90] John J. DiIulio, Jr., "Against Mandatory Minimums," *National Review*, May 17, 1999.

[91] U.S. Department of Justice, Bureau of Justice Statistics, "Substance Abuse and Treatment, State and Federal Prisoners, 1997."

[92] Ibid.

[93] Office of National Drug Control Policy, "Data Snapshot: Drug Abuse in America, 1998."

[94] Ibid.

[95] Ibid.

[96] Ibid.

[97] U.S. Department of Health and Human Services, Substance Abuse and Mental Health Statistics, "Drug Abuse Warning Network: Annual Trends in Total Drug-Related Episodes," 1996.

[98] U.S. Department of Health and Human Services, Substance Abuse and Mental Health Statistics, "1997 National Household Survey of Drug Abuse."

[99] U.S. Department of Justice, Bureau of Justice Statistics, "Alcohol and Crime," April 1999.

[100] Ibid.

[101] *USA Today*, "Traffic Deaths at Record Lows," May 28, 1999.

[102] Irvin Molotsky, "U.S. Cities Drop in Arrests for Drunken Driving," *New York Times*, June 14, 1999.

[103] U.S. Department of Justice, Bureau of Justice Statistics, *Sourcebook of Criminal Justice Statistics 1997* (Washington, DC: GPO, 1998).

[104] U.S. Department of Justice, Bureau of Justice Statistics, "Alcohol and Crime," April 1999.

CHAPTER TWO

Family

OUT-OF-WEDLOCK BIRTHS

- *Between 1990 and 1997, the percentage of births that are out of wedlock increased 16 percent. Between 1960 and 1997, the percentage increased 511 percent.*[1]

Out–of–Wedlock Births as a Percentage of All Births

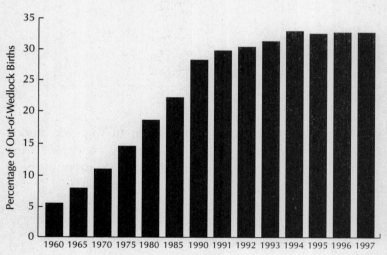

Source: National Center for Health Statistics

Out-of-Wedlock Births as a Percentage of All Births

Year	Percentage of Out-of-Wedlock Births	Out-of-Wedlock Births (total number)	Percentage of Out-of-Wedlock Births (white)
1960	5.3	224,300	2.3
1965	7.7	291,200	4.0
1970	10.7	398,700	5.7
1975	14.3	447,900	7.3
1980	18.4	665,747	11.2
1985	22.0	828,174	14.7
1990	28.0	1,165,384	20.4
1991	29.5	1,213,769	21.8
1992	30.1	1,224,876	22.6
1993	31.0	1,240,172	23.6
1994	32.6	1,289,592	25.5
1995	32.2	1,253,976	25.3
1996	32.4	1,260,306	25.7
1997	32.4	1,257,444	25.8

Source: National Center for Health Statistics

- The percentage of births that are out of wedlock among blacks increased 200 percent between 1960 and 1997. Currently, more than two-thirds of all black children are born out of wedlock.[2]

Percentage of Out–of–Wedlock Births Among Blacks

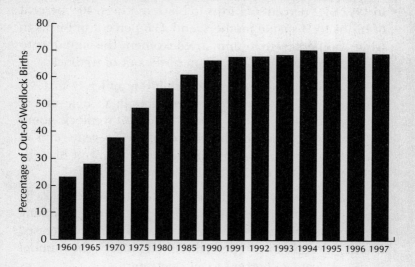

Percentage of Out–of–Wedlock Births Among Blacks

Year	Percentage of Out–of–Wedlock Births
1960	23.0
1965	27.9
1970	37.6
1975	48.8
1980	56.1
1985	61.2
1990	66.5
1991	67.9
1992	68.1
1993	68.7
1994	70.5
1995	69.9
1996	69.8
1997	69.2

Factual Overview: Out-of-Wedlock Births

- In 1997, 69.2 percent of births to black mothers, 40.9 percent of births to Hispanic mothers, and 25.8 percent of births to white mothers were to unmarried women. This amounts to a total of more than 1.25 million births out of wedlock.[3]

- Of the approximately 65 million children under 17 in 1996, almost 28 million (43 percent) spent time in a single–parent family. About 8.25 million were born out of wedlock, about 16.7 million experienced the divorce of their parents, and an additional 3 million or so children were born out of wed–lock *and* experienced the divorce of their parents.[4]

- In 1960, 5.3 percent of all births were out of wedlock. By 1997, that number had increased to 32.4 percent. Among whites, the percentage of out–of–wedlock births increased from 2.3 percent to 25.8 percent. Among blacks, the number increased from 23 percent to 69.2 percent.[5]

- In 1960, the number of children born out of wedlock was 224,300, and in 1997, the total number was more than 1.25 million.[6]

- Since 1960, there have been more than 25 million children born out of wedlock.[7]

- The overall fertility rate in the United States decreased by 45 percent between 1960 and 1997.[8]

- Of families with children under 18, the average number of children per family decreased from 2.33 in 1960 to 1.85 in 1998—a 21 percent decrease.[9]

- In 1997, there were 1,257,444 births to unmarried mothers. Of these, 385,802 (31 percent) were to women under age 20, while 673,394 (54 percent) of these unmarried births were to women in their 20s.[10]

- During the 1990s, the birth rate among married women has decreased by 10 percent (from 93.2 in 1990 to 84.3 in 1997), while the birth rate among unmarried women has increased slightly (from 43.8 to 44).[11]

Birth Rates, Married and Unmarried Women, 1990–97

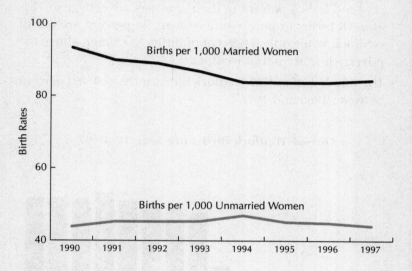

Birth Rates, Married and Unmarried Women, 1990–97

Year	Birth Rate (per 1,000 married women)	Birth Rate (per 1,000 unmarried women)
1990	93.2	43.8
1991	89.9	45.2
1992	89.0	45.2
1993	86.8	45.3
1994	83.8	46.9
1995	83.7	45.1
1996	83.7	44.8
1997	84.3	44.0

- While the birth rate among unmarried women was rising dramatically between 1960 and 1996, the birth rate within marriage was declining. Births to married women declined from 4 million in 1960 to 2.7 million in 1996, a 33 percent decrease.[12]

- Almost one-quarter of white births are to unmarried mothers—and only 4 percent of these mothers are college graduates. Of births to poor white women, 44 percent are out of wedlock, while only 6 percent of births to women above the poverty line are out of wedlock.[13]

- The number of out-of-wedlock births increased 460 percent between 1960 and 1997.[14]

Out-of-Wedlock Births per Year, 1960–97

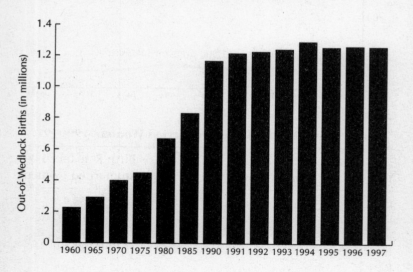

Out–of–Wedlock Births per Year, 1960–97

Year	Out-of-Wedlock Births
1960	224,300
1965	291,200
1970	398,700
1975	447,900
1980	665,747
1985	828,174
1990	1,165,384
1991	1,213,769
1992	1,224,876
1993	1,240,172
1994	1,289,592
1995	1,253,976
1996	1,260,306
1997	1,257,444

- In 1994, for the first time in American history, more than half of all firstborn children were conceived or born out of wedlock.[15]

First Births to Women

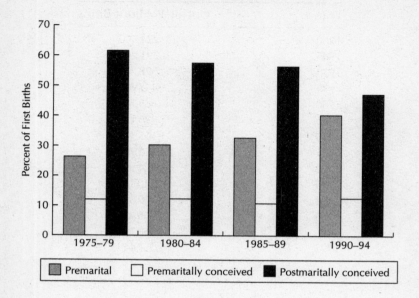

First Births to Women

Period	Percent of First Births That Were Premarital	Percent of First Births That Were Premaritally Conceived	Percent of First Births That Were Postmaritally Conceived
1975–79	26.4	12.0	61.6
1980–84	30.3	12.2	57.5
1985–89	32.7	10.8	56.4
1990–94	40.3	12.5	47.2

The States: Out-of-Wedlock Births

• The District of Columbia had the highest percentage of out-of-wedlock births in 1997, while Utah had the lowest percentage.[16]

Out–of–Wedlock Births
by State, 1997

State	Percent of Out–of–Wedlock Births
District of Columbia	63.6
Mississippi	45.4
Louisiana	43.9
New Mexico	43.5
South Carolina	38.0
Arizona	37.6
Delaware	36.0
Florida	36.0
Nevada	35.5
Georgia	35.4
New York	35.2
Arkansas	34.2
Tennessee	34.1
Alabama	33.9
Ohio	33.9
Maryland	33.5
Illinois	33.4
Michigan	33.2
Missouri	33.1
Rhode Island	33.1
California	32.8
Pennsylvania	32.8
Connecticut	32.7
Indiana	32.6
United States	**32.4**
Oklahoma	32.4
North Carolina	32.2
West Virginia	31.3
South Dakota	31.1

(continued next page)

State	Percent of Out-of-Wedlock Births
Texas	30.7
Alaska	30.6
Hawaii	29.9
Maine	29.7
Kentucky	29.5
Virginia	29.3
Oregon	28.8
Montana	28.7
Wisconsin	28.1
New Jersey	28.0
Kansas	27.6
Wyoming	27.4
Washington	27.1
Iowa	26.2
Vermont	26.1
North Dakota	26.0
Massachusetts	25.9
Nebraska	25.8
Colorado	25.2
Minnesota	25.0
New Hampshire	23.8
Idaho	20.7
Utah	16.6

SINGLE-PARENT FAMILIES

- *Between 1990 and 1998, the percentage of families that are headed by a single parent increased 13 percent. Between 1960 and 1998, the percentage of single-parent families more than tripled.*[17]

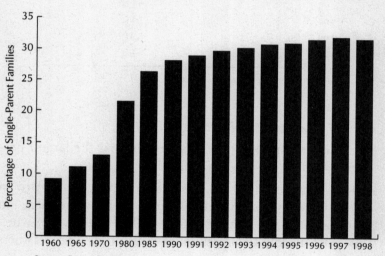

Single–Parent Families as a Percentage of All Families

Source: Census Bureau

Single–Parent Families as a Percentage of All Families

Year	Single–Parent Families (percent)
1960	9.1
1965	11.0
1970	12.9
1975	NA
1980	21.5
1985	26.3
1990	28.1
1991	28.9
1992	29.7
1993	30.2
1994	30.8
1995	31.0
1996	31.6
1997	32.0
1998	31.7

Source: Census Bureau

Factual Overview: Single-Parent Families

- Among industrialized nations, America has the largest percentage of single–parent families.[18]

- More than one–third (36 percent) of American children in 1990 were living apart from their biological fathers, an increase from 17.5 percent in 1960. Unlike earlier years, when paternal death rates were higher, most of the absent fathers today are alive.[19]

- Today, only about 50 percent of children will spend their entire childhood in an intact family.[20]

- Of the more than 71 million children in the United States, almost one–third do not live in a two–parent family.[21]

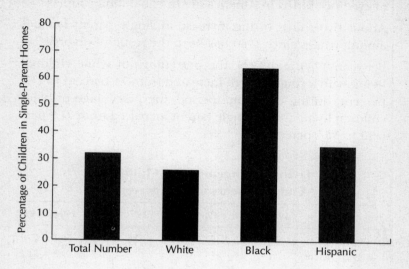

Percentage of Children Living in Single–Parent Families, 1998

Living Arrangements of Children, 1998

	Total Number	White	Black	Hispanic
Total children	71,377,000	56,124,000	11,414,000	10,863,000
Two parents	48,642,000	41,547,000	4,137,000	6,909,000
Mother only	16,634,000	10,210,000	5,830,000	2,915,000
Father only	3,143,000	2,562,000	424,000	482,000
Percent not in two-parent family	32	26	64	35

- Nearly 80 percent of black women will be the head of the family at some point in their childbearing years.[22]

- Mothers head 84 percent of single–parent families, while father–only households make up 16 percent.[23]

- Unlike European nations, in which most out–of–wedlock births are to cohabiting couples, most nonmarital births in

America are to unattached women. About 27 percent of out–of–wedlock births in America are to cohabiting couples.[24]

- About two–thirds of the increase in single–parent families among whites since 1960 has been the result of divorce.[25]

- Between 1960 and 1995, the percentage of white children living with a single parent increased from 7.1 percent to 21.2 percent; during that same period, the percentage of black children living with a single parent increased from 21.9 percent to 56.1 percent.[26]

Living Arrangements of Children Under 18 Years of Age (percent)

	1960	1970	1980	1990	1991	1993	1994	1995
White, two–parent	90.9	89.5	82.7	79.0	78.5	77.2	76.2	75.8
White, single parent	7.1	8.7	15.1	19.2	19.5	20.9	20.9	21.2
White, living with other relative or nonrelative	1.9	1.8	2.2	1.8	2.0	1.9	2.9	3.0
Black, two–parent	67.0	58.5	42.2	37.7	35.9	35.6	33.3	33.1
Black, single parent	21.9	31.8	45.8	54.8	57.5	57.0	57.1	56.1
Black, living with other relative or nonrelative	11.1	9.7	12.0	7.5	6.5	7.4	9.5	10.8

- About 40 percent of the children who live in fatherless households have not seen their fathers in at least a year.[27]

- The median family income for two–parent families is more than double that of families in which the mother is divorced and more than four times as much as that of families in which the mother never married.[28]

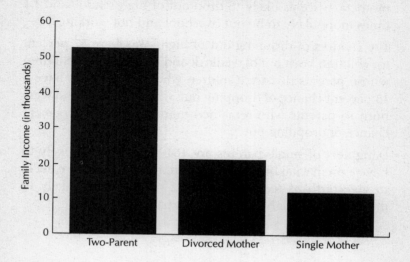

Median Family Income, 1998

Family Type	Median Family Income
Two-parent	$52,553
Divorced mother	21,316
Single mother	12,064

- Seventy-two percent of America's adolescent murderers, 70 percent of long-term prison inmates, and 60 percent of rapists come from fatherless homes.[29]
- Children who grow up with only one of their biological parents, when compared to children who grow up with both biological parents, are three times more likely to have a child

out of wedlock, 2.5 times more likely to become teenage mothers, twice as likely to drop out of high school, and 1.4 times more likely to be out of school and not working.[30]

- The chances of dropping out of high school are 37 percent for children born out of wedlock and 31 percent for children whose parents divorce. Children whose father died have a 15 percent chance of dropping out, while children who were born to parents who remained married have a 13 percent chance of dropping out.[31]

- Daughters of single parents are 164 percent more likely to have a premarital birth of their own, 111 percent more likely to give birth as teenagers, and 92 percent more likely to divorce than daughters of married parents.[32]

MARRIAGE AND COHABITATION

- *Between 1990 and 1997, the marriage rate has decreased 9 percent. Between 1960 and 1997, the rate decreased by 33 percent.*[33]

Marriage Rate

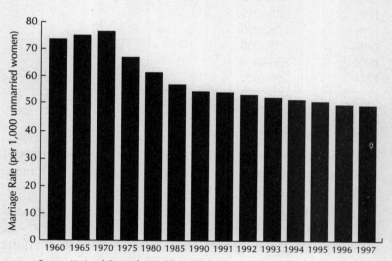

Source: National Center for Health Statistics

Number and Rate of Marriages

Year	Marriages (total number)	Marriage Rate (per 1,000 unmarried women)
1960	1,523,000	73.5
1965	1,800,000	75.0
1970	2,159,000	76.5
1975	2,153,000	66.9
1980	2,390,000	61.4
1985	2,413,000	57.0
1990	2,443,000	54.5
1991	2,371,000	54.2
1992	2,362,000	53.3
1993	2,334,000	52.3
1994	2,362,000	51.5
1995	2,336,000	50.8
1996	2,344,000	49.7
1997	2,384,000	49.4

Source: National Center for Health Statistics

Factual Overview: Marriage

- In 1960, married couples made up almost three–quarters of all households. By 1998, married couples were just more than half of all households.[34]

- The percentage of adults who have never married increased from 20.3 percent in 1980 to 23.5 percent in 1997—an increase of 16 percent. For blacks, the percentage of adults who have never married increased 28 percent, from 30.5 percent in 1980 to 39.1 percent in 1997.[35]

Factual Overview: Cohabitation

- The number of cohabiting couples increased from 439,000 in 1960 to 4.24 million in 1998—an almost tenfold increase.

During the 1990s, the number of cohabiting households increased by almost 50 percent.[36]

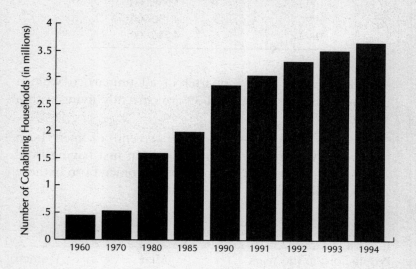

Cohabiting Households, 1960–98

Cohabiting Households, 1960–98

Year	Cohabiting Households (total number)
1960	439,000
1970	523,000
1980	1,589,000
1985	1,983,000
1990	2,856,000
1991	3,039,000
1992	3,308,000
1993	3,510,000

(continued next page)

Year	Cohabiting Households (total number)
1994	3,661,000
1995	3,668,000
1996	3,958,000
1997	4,130,000
1998	4,236,000

- Studies indicate that a quarter of all unmarried women between the ages of 25 and 39 are currently living with a partner.[37]

- Just more than one-third (33.9 percent) of men born between 1963 and 1974 married without first having lived with their partner, and 35.3 percent of women born in those years married without first cohabiting.[38]

Percentage of Marriages Without Prior Cohabitation

People Born in the Years	Men	Women
1933–42	84.5	93.8
1943–52	66.7	75.7
1953–62	46.6	57.3
1963–72	33.9	35.3

- In 1980, there were 431,000 households with unmarried couples with children under 15 years of age; in 1997, there were 1,470,000.[39]

- Among households with cohabiting adults between the ages of 25 and 34, the percentage with children increased from 34 percent in 1980 to 47 percent in 1990.[40]

- The poverty rate in 1996 for children living in married-couple households was 6 percent, but 31 percent for children in cohabiting households—much closer to the rate of 45 percent for families headed by single mothers.[41]

- Virtually all research has concluded that the chances of divorce are significantly greater for couples who cohabit before marriage than for those who do not.[42] Indeed, couples who cohabitate before marriage are almost twice as likely to divorce as those who do not.[43]

- Cohabiting couples report more disagreements, more frequent fights, and lower levels of happiness than married couples.[44]

Factual Overview: Stepfamilies

- One of every six children is a stepchild.[45]

- More than nine out of ten stepchildren are in families with their biological mother and a stepfather.[46]

- More than half of all stepfamilies divorce within ten years.[47]

- While remarriage brings additional income into the household, the children in stepfamilies have as many behavioral problems as children in single-parent families.[48]

DIVORCE

- *Between 1990 and 1997, the divorce rate decreased by 5 percent. But between 1960 and 1997, the divorce rate more than doubled.*[49]

Divorce Rate

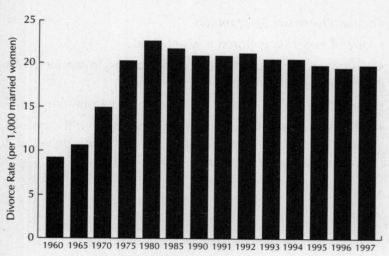

Source: National Center for Health Statistics

Number and Rate of Divorces

Year	Divorces (total number)	Divorce Rate (per 1,000 married women)
1960	393,000	9.2
1965	479,000	10.6
1970	708,000	14.9
1975	1,036,000	20.3
1980	1,189,000	22.6
1985	1,190,000	21.7
1990	1,182,000	20.9
1991	1,189,000	20.9
1992	1,215,000	21.2
1993	1,187,000	20.5
1994	1,191,000	20.5
1995	1,169,000	19.8
1996	1,150,000	19.5
1997	1,163,000	19.8

Source: National Center for Health Statistics

Factual Overview: Divorce and Adultery

- Today, forty out of every one hundred first marriages end in divorce, compared to sixteen out of every one hundred first marriages in 1960.[50]

- America has the highest divorce rate of Western nations.[51]

Divorce Rate by Nation, 1960 and 1990

Country	1960	1990
United States	**9**	**21**
Denmark	6	13
Sweden	5	12

(continued next page)

Country	1960	1990
Canada	2	12
United Kingdom	2	12
Germany	4	8
France	3	8
Netherlands	2	8
Italy	1	2

- Much of the decrease in the number of divorces during the 1990s can be attributed to the increase of couples cohabiting and the decrease in the number of marriages.[52]

- In America today, almost one of every ten adults (9.8 percent) is divorced, which is more than three times what the number was in 1970 (3.2 percent).[53]

- Between 1960 and 1997, the rate of divorce more than doubled, while the marriage rate declined by almost one-third.[54]

Marriage and Divorce Rates, 1960–97

Year	Marriage Rate (per 1,000 unmarried women)	Divorce Rate (per 1,000 married women)
1960	73.5	9.2
1970	76.5	14.9
1980	61.4	22.6
1990	54.5	20.9
1991	54.2	20.9
1992	53.3	21.2
1993	52.3	20.5
1994	51.5	20.5
1995	50.8	19.8
1996	49.7	19.5
1997	49.4	19.8

- Slightly more than 20 percent of men and about 11 percent of women have been unfaithful to their spouse at least once in their life. When asked, 3.6 percent of men and 1.3 percent of women admit having committed adultery in the last year.[55]

Factual Overview: Divorce and Children

- The odds that a child today will witness the divorce of his or her parents are one in two. A generation ago, the odds were one in four.[56]

- The number of children involved in divorce was 463,000 in 1960, but rose to 1.05 million in 1995.[57]

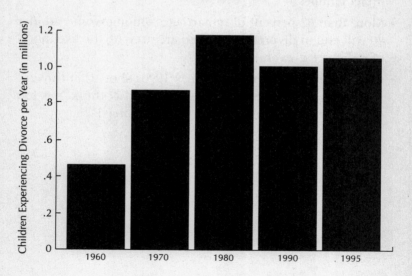

Number of Children Experiencing Divorce per Year, 1960–95

**Number of Children Experiencing
Divorce per Year, 1960–95**

Year	Number of Children
1960	463,000
1970	870,000
1980	1,174,000
1990	1,005,000
1995	1,052,000

- Currently, about three of five divorcing couples have at least one child.[58]

- Children whose parents are divorced are more likely to exhibit conduct problems, psychological maladjustment, and lower academic achievement. They are also more likely to drop out of school, engage in premarital sex, and become pregnant outside of marriage, compared to children in intact families.[59]

- More than 62 percent of remarriages among women under 40 will end in divorce. If children are present, the likelihood of redivorce is even higher.[60]

- Gallup youth surveys in the early 1990s show that three of four teenagers between the ages of 13 and 17 think "it is too easy for people in this country to get divorced."[61]

CHILD WELL-BEING

- *Between 1990 and 1996, the percentage of children in poverty* stayed about the same. Overall, between 1970 and 1996, the percentage of children in poverty increased by one-third.*[62]

Percentage of Children in Poverty

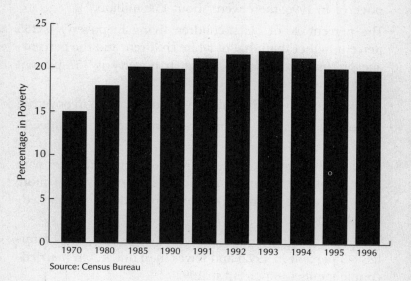

Source: Census Bureau

* Children in poverty are related children in families with an annual income below the poverty level. In 1997, the poverty level was $16,400 for a family of four (U.S. Department of Commerce, Bureau of the Census, "Poverty in the United States: 1997").

Children in Poverty

	1970	1980	1985	1990	1991	1992	1993	1994	1995	1996
Total (in millions)	10.2	11.1	12.5	12.7	13.7	14.5	15.0	14.6	14.0	13.8
Total percent	14.9	17.9	20.1	19.9	21.1	21.6	22.0	21.2	20.0	19.8

Source: Census Bureau

Factual Overview: Child Poverty

- The child poverty rate in the United States is among the highest in the industrialized world.[63]

- In 1993, there were almost 15 million children under 18 in poverty. In 1996, there were about 13.8 million.[64]

- The percentage of black children living in poverty is 155 percent higher than that of white children, and the percentage of Hispanic children living in poverty is 157 percent higher than that of white children.[65]

- Almost one of every five children in America lives in poverty.[66]

- About 40 percent of all Americans in poverty are under 18 years old.[67]

- Almost 60 percent of children under 6 living in families with only a mother had an income below the poverty level, more than five times as many as children under 6 in married-couple families (10.6 percent).[68]

- Poverty afflicts nearly one of every two mother–only families (45 percent in 1992) and fewer than one in ten married-couple families (8 percent in 1992).[69]

Factual Overview: Child Abuse

- In 1997, there were 3 million reports of child abuse and neglect—more than double 1986's 1.4 million reports.[70]

- The overwhelming number of perpetrators of sexual abuse against children are male, comprising an estimated 95 percent of girl abusers and 80 percent of boy abusers.[71]
- Children whose parents abuse drugs and alcohol are almost three times likelier to be physically or sexually assaulted and more than four times likelier to be neglected than children of parents who are not substance abusers.[72]
- Substance abuse causes or is a directly contributing factor in seven out of ten cases of child abuse or neglect.[73]
- Parents with alcohol and drug problems are more than twice as likely to abuse or neglect children repeatedly, compared to families with no apparent substance abuse problem (58 percent vs. 25 percent).[74]
- Parents under the influence of illegal drugs and/or alcohol are responsible for as many as two-thirds of deaths due to child abuse or neglect.[75]

Factual Overview: Child Care

- About 77 percent of preschoolers are cared for by their parents or other family members, while about 15 percent are in day-care centers; the remaining 8 percent are cared for by baby-sitters or other nonrelatives (most of whom are unlicensed).[76]
- In 1996, 47.5 percent of mothers with children under 18 worked full-time, and 19 percent worked part-time. For mothers with children under 6, 39 percent worked full-time and 19.1 percent worked part-time.[77]
- More than 66 percent of divorced mothers with children under 18 work full-time, compared to 35.5 percent of never-married mothers.[78]
- Children in poor families are more likely to be cared for by relatives than children in nonpoor families.[79]

WELFARE

- *Between 1990 and 1998, the percentage of Americans receiving AFDC/TANF payments decreased 39 percent. But overall, between 1960 and 1998, the percentage increased 65 percent.*[80]

Percentage of American Population on AFDC/TANF

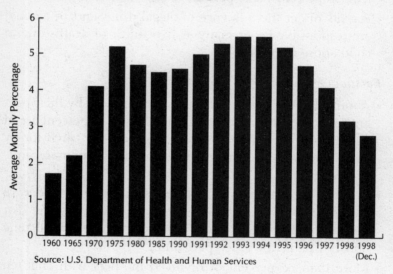

Source: U.S. Department of Health and Human Services

Number and Percentage of Americans on AFDC/TANF

Year	Average Number of Monthly Recipients	Average Monthly Percentage of Population on Welfare
1960	3,005,000	1.7
1965	4,329,000	2.2
1970	8,466,000	4.1
1975	11,165,185	5.2
1980	10,597,445	4.7
1985	10,812,625	4.5
1990	11,460,382	4.6
1991	12,592,269	5.0
1992	13,625,342	5.3
1993	14,142,710	5.5
1994	14,225,591	5.5
1995	13,652,232	5.2
1996	12,648,859	4.7
1997	10,936,298	4.1
1998	8,770,376	3.2
December 1998	7,612,941	2.8

Source: U.S. Department of Health and Human Services

Factual Overview: Welfare

- Between 1994, when welfare rolls were at their peak, and 1998, the number of people receiving monthly welfare payments has decreased 46.5 percent.[81]

- There was a 22 percent increase in the number of households receiving food stamps between 1980 and 1996.[82]

- Of the five states that saw the greatest decrease in welfare rolls between 1994 and 1997, four saw an increase in the out–of–wedlock birth rate during that same period.[83]

• The number of households receiving means-tested noncash benefits increased 52 percent between 1980 and 1996. The percentage of households receiving those benefits also increased (by 23.7 percent) in that period.[84]

• In 1961, there were 2,665,388 children on welfare. At the peak of welfare enrollment in 1994, there were 9,464,187. At the end of 1997, there were 5,489,183.[85]

• A study by Wisconsin's Department of Workforce Development indicated that more than 62 percent of former Wisconsin welfare recipients were employed within five months of leaving the welfare rolls. Most were working full-time, and the average wage was $7.42 an hour.[86]

The States: Decline in Caseloads

• In August 1996, welfare reform legislation (passed in 1994) took effect. Between 1996 and 1998, the United States has seen an overall decrease of 38 percent in welfare caseloads.[87]

Welfare Caseload Decline by State, 1996–98

State	August 1996	December 1998	Percent Decrease
Idaho	21,780	3,128	86
Wyoming	11,398	1,913	83
Wisconsin	148,888	33,807	77
West Virginia	89,039	27,529	69
Mississippi	123,828	43,499	65
Florida	533,801	227,156	57
South Carolina	114,273	49,383	57
Colorado	95,788	41,674	56
Georgia	330,302	154,900	53
Alabama	100,662	49,461	51

(continued next page)

State	August 1996	December 1998	Percent Decrease
Texas	649,018	330,616	49
Maryland	194,127	99,852	49
Delaware	23,654	12,316	48
Arkansas	56,343	30,606	46
Montana	29,130	16,133	45
Michigan	502,354	279,245	44
North Carolina	267,326	148,782	44
Louisiana	228,115	128,016	44
Oregon	78,419	44,126	44
South Dakota	15,896	8,945	44
Arizona	169,442	96,298	43
Ohio	549,312	319,912	42
Oklahoma	96,201	55,531	42
Tennessee	254,818	149,138	41
Pennsylvania	531,059	325,546	39
Kentucky	172,193	104,683	39
U.S, average	**12,241,489**	**7,612,941**	**38**
Missouri	222,820	137,954	38
Connecticut	159,246	97,600	38
Virginia	152,845	94,383	38
North Dakota	13,146	8,359	36
Illinois	642,644	414,872	35
New Jersey	275,637	179,910	35
Washington	268,927	178,333	34
Massachusetts	226,030	150,641	33
Nevada	34,261	23,108	33
Hawaii	66,482	45,452	32
Maine	53,873	36,870	32
New Hampshire	22,937	15,893	31
Iowa	86,146	59,945	30
Utah	39,073	27,526	30
California	2,581,948	1,850,898	28

(continued next page)

State	August 1996	December 1998	Percent Decrease
Alaska	35,544	25,472	28
New York	1,143,962	833,045	27
Vermont	24,331	18,260	25
District of Columbia	69,292	53,455	23
Indiana	142,604	113,680	20
Minnesota	169,744	138,030	19
New Mexico	99,661	80,583	19
Nebraska	38,592	34,809	10
Rhode Island	56,560	54,175	4

ABORTION

- *Between 1990 and 1996, the abortion ratio* decreased 7 percent. But overall, between 1973 and 1996, the ratio increased 35 percent.*[88]

Abortion Ratio

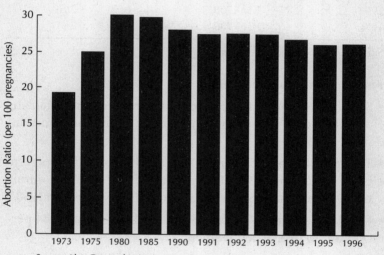

Source: Alan Guttmacher Institute

* For a discussion of the difference between rates and ratios, please see the "Note to the Reader" in the back of the book.

Number and Ratio of Abortions

Year	Abortions (total number)	Abortion Ratio* (per 100 pregnancies)
1973	744,600	19.3
1975	1,034,200	24.9
1980	1,553,900	30.0
1985	1,588,600	29.7
1990	1,608,600	28.0
1991	1,556,500	27.4
1992	1,528,900	27.5
1993	1,500,000	27.4
1994	1,431,000	26.7
1995	1,363,700	26.0
1996	1,365,700	26.1

Source: Alan Guttmacher Institute

Factual Overview: Abortion

- Since *Roe v. Wade*, the Supreme Court decision legalizing abortion, there have been more than 35 million abortions performed.[89]

- The rate of abortions per 1,000 women increased 40 percent between 1973 and 1996. The rate has fallen 16 percent during the 1990s and has decreased 22 percent from its peak in 1980.[90]

- Of all the abortions performed in the United States, 84 percent are to unmarried women.[91]

- Women in their 20s account for more than half of all abortions performed annually.[92]

---

* The abortion ratio is defined in terms of abortions per 100 pregnancies, not including those that end in miscarriages.

Abortions by Age, 1995

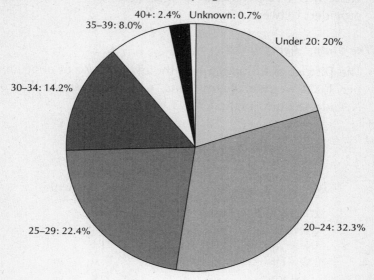

- White women obtain 60 percent of all abortions, but the abortion rate for black women is three times higher than that for white women, while the abortion rate for Hispanic women is twice as high as that for white women.[93]

- Every year, about 6 million women become pregnant. Almost half of all pregnancies in America are unintended— and half of these unintended pregnancies are terminated by abortion.[94]

- Only 7 percent of all abortions fall into the category of threatened life of the mother, fetal deformity, or victim of rape or incest.[95]

- More than 54 percent of all abortions occur within the first eight weeks of pregnancy, and 1.5 percent occur after the twenty-first week.[96]

- There was a 14 percent decline in the number of abortion providers between 1992 and 1996.[97]

The States: Abortion Rates

- The District of Columbia had the highest rate of abortions per 1,000 women of any state, more than triple that of Nevada, the next highest.[98]

Abortion Rates by State, 1996

State	Abortion Rate (per 1,000 women)
District of Columbia	154.5
Nevada	44.6
New York	41.1
New Jersey	35.8
California	33.0
Florida	32.0
Massachusetts	29.3
Hawaii	27.3
Maryland	26.3
Illinois	26.1
Rhode Island	24.4
Delaware	24.1
United States	**22.9**
Connecticut	22.5
Michigan	22.3
Oregon	21.6
Georgia	21.1
Colorado	20.9
Washington	20.9
Texas	20.7
North Carolina	20.2

(continued next page)

State	Abortion Rate (per 1,000 women)
Arizona	19.8
Kansas	18.9
Virginia	18.9
Vermont	17.1
Ohio	17.0
Montana	15.6
Alabama	15.6
Pennsylvania	15.2
Tennessee	14.8
Louisiana	14.7
Alaska	14.6
New Mexico	14.4
Minnesota	13.9
New Hampshire	12.7
Nebraska	12.3
Wisconsin	12.3
Oklahoma	11.8
South Carolina	11.6
Arkansas	11.4
Indiana	11.2
Maine	9.7
Kentucky	9.6
Iowa	9.4
North Dakota	9.4
Missouri	9.1
Utah	7.8
Mississippi	7.2
West Virginia	6.6
South Dakota	6.5
Idaho	6.1
Wyoming	2.7

Factual Overview: Sexually Transmitted Diseases

- The United States' gonorrhea rate is several times higher than rates in other developed countries.[99]

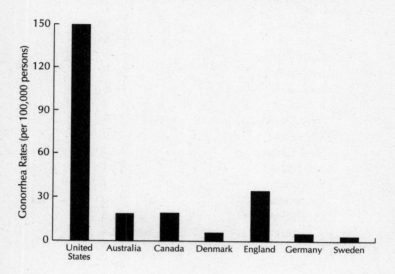

Gonorrhea Rates in Developed Countries, 1995

- The rates of some sexually transmitted diseases in America far exceed those of every other developed country and are even greater than those in some developing countries.[100]
- The number of Americans with AIDS decreased from 103,228 in 1993 to 46,311 in 1998—a decrease of 55 percent.[101]
- There are approximately 45 million Americans with genital herpes and 20 million Americans with the human papillomavirus (HPV) infection.[102]

Sexually Transmitted Disease Rates
in Developed Countries, 1995

Country	Syphilis Rate (per 100,000 persons)	Gonorrhea Rate (per 100,000 persons)
United States	**6.3**	**149.5**
Australia	NA	18.1
Canada	0.4	18.6
Denmark	0.4	5.5
England	1.0	34.1
Germany	1.4	4.9
Sweden	0.8	3.0

- Researchers estimate that there are approximately 15.3 million new cases of sexually transmitted diseases each year.[103]

- In a single act of unprotected sex with an infected partner, a teenage girl has a 1 percent risk of acquiring HIV, a 30 percent risk of getting genital herpes, and a 50 percent chance of contracting gonorrhea.[104]

- Among the top ten most frequently reported diseases in 1995 in the United States, sexually transmitted diseases accounted for 87 percent.[105]

NOTES

[1] U.S. Department of Health and Human Services, National Center for Health Statistics, "Births to Unmarried Mothers: United States, 1980–92," and assorted Monthly Vital Statistics Reports.

[2] Ibid.

[3] Ibid.

[4] Bureau of Labor Statistics, National Longitudinal Survey of Youth, 1996 Cohort.

[5] U.S. Department of Health and Human Services, National Center for Health Statistics, "Births to Unmarried Mothers: United States, 1980–92," and "National Vital Statistics Report," Vol. 47, No. 4.

[6] U.S. Department of Health and Human Services, National Center for Health Statistics, assorted Monthly Vital Statistics Reports.

[7] U.S. Department of Health and Human Services, National Center for Health Statistics, "Births to Unmarried Mothers: United States, 1980–92," and assorted Monthly Vital Statistics Reports.

[8] U.S. Department of Health and Human Services, National Center for Health Statistics, "Monthly Vital Statistics Report," Vol. 45, No. 11 (S), and "National Vital Statistics Report," Vol. 47, No. 18.

[9] U.S. Department of Commerce, Bureau of the Census, "Average Number of Own Children under 18 per Family, by Type of Family: 1955 to Present."

[10] U.S. Department of Health and Human Services, National Center for Health Statistics, "National Vital Statistics Report" Vol. 47, No. 18.

[11] U.S. Department of Health and Human Services, National Center for Health Statistics, "National Vital Statistics Report," Vol. 47, No. 18.

[12] Federal Interagency Forum on Child and Family Statistics, "America's Children 1998: Population and Family Characteristics."

[13] Ed Rubenstein, "200 Years and Out," *National Review* 4 (April 1994). Cited in National Fatherhood Initiative, *Father Facts*, 1998.

[14] U.S. Department of Health and Human Services, National Center for Health Statistics, "Births to Unmarried Mothers: United States, 1980–92," and assorted Monthly Vital Statistics Reports.

[15] U.S. Department of Commerce, Bureau of the Census, "Marital Status of Women at First Birth: 1930–34 to 1990–94."

[16] U.S. Department of Health and Human Services, National Center for Health Statistics, "National Vital Statistics Report," Vol. 47, No. 18.

[17] U.S. Department of Commerce, Bureau of the Census, "All Parent/Child Situations by Type, Race, and Hispanic Origin."

[18] Sara McLanahan and Gary Sandefur, *Growing Up with a Single Parent* (Cambridge: Harvard UP, 1996).

[19] Council on Families in America, *Marriage in America: A Report to the Nation*, 1995.

[20] David Popenoe, "American Family Decline, 1960–1990: A Review and Appraisal," *Journal of Marriage and the Family* 55 (August 1993). Cited in National Fatherhood Initiative, *Father Facts*, 1998.

[21] U.S. Department of Commerce, Bureau of the Census, "Marital Status and Living Arrangements: March 1998."

[22] Robert A. Moffitt and Michael S. Rendall, "Cohort Trends in the Lifetime

Distribution of Female Family Headship in the United States, 1968–1985," *Demography* 32 (August 1995). Cited in National Fatherhood Initiative, *Father Facts*, 1998.

[23] U.S. Department of Commerce, Bureau of the Census, "Living Arrangements of Children under 18 Years Old: 1960 to Present."

[24] David Popenoe, *Life Without Father* (New York: The Free Press, 1996).

[25] Irwin Garfinkel and Sara S. McLanahan, *Single Mothers and Their Children: A New American Dilemma* (Washington, DC: Urban Institute, 1989). Cited in National Fatherhood Initiative, *Father Facts*, 1998.

[26] U.S. Congress, Committee on Ways and Means, *The Green Book* (Washington, DC: GPO, 1996); U.S. Bureau of the Census, *Statistical Abstract of the United States 1997* (Washington, DC: GPO, 1997). Cited in National Fatherhood Initiative, *Father Facts*, 1998.

[27] National Fatherhood Initiative, *Father Facts*, 1998.

[28] U.S. Department of Commerce, Bureau of the Census, "Marital Status and Living Arrangements: March 1998."

[29] David Popenoe, *Life Without Father* (New York: The Free Press, 1996).

[30] Ibid.

[31] Sara McLanahan and Gary Sandefur, *Growing Up with a Single Parent* (Cambridge: Harvard UP, 1996).

[32] Irwin Garfinkel and Sara McLanahan, *Single Mothers and Their Children* (Washington, DC: Urban Institute Press, 1989). Cited in National Fatherhood Initiative, *Father Facts*, 1998.

[33] U.S. Department of Commerce, Bureau of the Census, *Statistical Abstract of the United States 1998* (Washington, DC: GPO, 1998), and U.S. Department of Health and Human Services, "Monthly Vital Statistics Report," Vol. 43, No. 12, and Vol. 46, No. 12.

[34] U.S. Department of Commerce, Bureau of the Census, "Households by Type: 1940 to Present."

[35] U.S. Department of Commerce, Bureau of the Census, *Statistical Abstract of the United States 1998* (Washington, DC: GPO, 1998).

[36] U.S. Department of Commerce, Bureau of the Census, "Unmarried-Couple Households, by Presence of Children: 1960 to Present."

[37] David Popenoe and Barbara Dafoe Whitehead, "Should We Live Together?" (New Brunswick, NJ: National Marriage Project, January 1999).

[38] Robert T. Michael et al. *Sex in America: A Definitive Survey* (New York: Little, Brown & Co., 1994).

[39] U.S. Department of Commerce, Bureau of the Census, *Statistical Abstract of the United States 1998* (Washington, DC: GPO, 1998).

[40] U.S. Department of Commerce, Bureau of the Census, *Statistical Abstract*

of the United States 1996 (Washington, DC: GPO, 1996). Cited in National Fatherhood Initiative, *Father Facts,* 1998.

[41] David Popenoe and Barbara Dafoe Whitehead, "Should We Live Together?" (New Brunswick, NJ: National Marriage Project, January 1999).

[42] Ibid.

[43] Alfred DeMaris and K. Vaninadha Rao, "Premarital Cohabitation and Subsequent Marital Stability in the United States: A Reassessment," *Journal of Marriage and the Family* 54 (1992). Cited in David Popenoe and Barbara Dafoe Whitehead, "Should We Live Together?" (New Brunswick, NJ: National Marriage Project, January 1999).

[44] Susan L. Brown and Alan Booth, "Cohabitation versus Marriage: A Comparison of Relationship Quality," *Journal of Marriage and Family* 58 (August 1996). Cited in National Fatherhood Initiative, *Father Facts,* 1998.

[45] Camille Sweeny, "Portrait of the American Child, 1995," *New York Times,* October 8, 1995.

[46] David Popenoe, "The Evolution of Marriage and the Problem of Step-families: A Biosocial Perspective," in Alan Booth and Judy Dunn, eds., *Stepfamilies: Who Benefits? Who Does Not?* (Mahwah, NJ: Lawrence Erlbaum, 1994).

[47] Larry L. Bumpass, R. Kelly Raley, and James A. Sweet, "The Changing Character of Stepfamilies: Implications of Cohabitation and Nonmarital Childbearing," *Demography* 32 (August 1995).

[48] James H. Bray, "Children's Development during Early Remarriage," in E. M. Hetherington and J. D. Arasteh, eds., *Impact of Divorce, Single Parenting, and Stepparenting on Children* (Hillsdale: Erlbaum, 1988), Kathleen Kiernan, "The Impact of Family Disruption in Childhood on Transitions Made in Young Adult Life," *Population Studies* 46 (1992), and David Popenoe, "The Evolution of Marriage and the Problem of Stepfamilies," National Symposium on Stepfamilies, Pennsylvania State University, University Park, PA, October 1993. Cited in National Fatherhood Initiative, *Father Facts,* 1998.

[49] U.S. Department of Commerce, Bureau of the Census, *Statistical Abstract of the United States 1998* (Washington, DC: GPO, 1998), and U.S. Department of Health and Human Services, National Center for Health Statistics, "Monthly Vital Statistics Report," Vol. 46, No. 12, and Vol. 43, No. 9 (S).

[50] Wade Horn, "Did You Say 'Movement'?" *American Experiment Quarterly,* Winter 1998–99.

[51] Sara McLanahan and Gary Sandefur, *Growing Up with a Single Parent* (Cambridge: Harvard UP, 1996).

[52] David Popenoe, *Life Without Father* (New York: The Free Press, 1996).

[53] U.S. Department of Commerce, Bureau of the Census, "Marital Status and Living Arrangements: March 1994" and "Marital Status and Living Arrangements: March 1998."

[54] U.S. Department of Commerce, Bureau of the Census, *Statistical Abstract of the United States 1998* (Washington, DC: GPO, 1998), and U.S. Department of Health and Human Services, National Center for Health Statistics, "Monthly Vital Statistics Report," Vol. 43, No. 9 (S), Vol. 45, No. 12, and Vol. 46, No. 12.

[55] National Opinion Research Center, cited in Jerry Adler, "Adultery: A New Furor Over an Old Sin," *Newsweek*, September 30, 1996.

[56] Larry L. Bumpass, "What's Happening to the Family: Interactions between Demographics and Institutional Change," *Demography* 27.4 (1990): Cited in National Fatherhood Initiative, *Father Facts*, 1998.

[57] National Fatherhood Initiative, *Father Facts*, 1998.

[58] Larry L. Bumpass, "What's Happening to the Family: Interactions between Demographics and Institutional Change," *Demography* 27.4 (1990). Cited in National Fatherhood Initiative, *Father Facts*, 1998.

[59] Paul R. Amato, "Life-Span Adjustment of Children to Their Parents' Divorce," *Future of Children* 4.1 (Spring 1994), Frank F. Furstenberg, Jr., and Julien O. Teitler, "Reconsidering the Effects of Marital Disruption: What Happens to Children of Divorce in Early Adulthood?" *Journal of Family Issues* 15 (1994). Cited in National Fatherhood Initiative, *Father Facts*, 1998.

[60] David Popenoe, "The Evolution of Marriage and the Problem of Stepfamilies: A Biosocial Perspective," in Alan Booth and Judy Dunn, eds., *Stepfamilies: Who Benefits? Who Does Not?* (Mahwah, NJ: Lawrence Erlbaum, 1994).

[61] Karl Zinsmeister, "Divorce's Toll on Children," *American Enterprise*, Vol. 7, No. 3 (May/June 1996).

[62] U.S. Department of Commerce, Bureau of the Census, *Statistical Abstract of the United States 1998* (Washington, DC: GPO, 1998).

[63] Annie E. Casey Foundation, "Kids Count," 1999.

[64] U.S. Department of Commerce, Bureau of the Census, *Statistical Abstract of the United States 1998* (Washington, DC: GPO, 1998).

[65] Ibid.

[66] U.S. Department of Commerce, Bureau of the Census, "Poverty in the United States: 1997."

[67] Ibid.

[68] Ibid.

[69] David Popenoe, *Life Without Father* (New York: The Free Press, 1996).

[70] National Center on Addiction and Substance Abuse at Columbia University, "No Safe Haven: Children of Substance Abusing Parents," 1998.

[71] David Popenoe, *Life Without Father* (New York: The Free Press, 1996).

[72] National Center on Addiction and Substance Abuse at Columbia University, "No Safe Haven: Children of Substance Abusing Parents," 1998.

[73] Ibid.

[74] Ibid.

[75] Ibid.

[76] David Blankenhorn, "Shouldn't We Help Parents Be Parents?" *New York Times*, December 19, 1997.

[77] U.S. Congress, House Ways and Means Committee, *The Green Book* (Washington, DC: GPO, 1998).

[78] Ibid.

[79] Ibid.

[80] U.S. Department of Health and Human Services, Administration for Children and Families, April 1999.

[81] Ibid.

[82] U.S. Department of Commerce, Bureau of the Census, *Statistical Abstract of the United States 1998* (Washington, DC: GPO, 1998).

[83] Heritage Foundation, "State Trends in Illegitimacy Ratios."

[84] U.S. Department of Commerce, Bureau of the Census, *Statistical Abstract of the United States 1998* (Washington, DC: GPO, 1998).

[85] U.S. Department of Health and Human Services, Office of Family Assistance, assorted reports.

[86] Cheryl Wetzstein, "Reform Works, Study Claims," *Washington Times*, May 13, 1999.

[87] U.S. Department of Health and Human Services, Administration for Children and Families, April 1999.

[88] Alan Guttmacher Institute, "Abortion Incidence and Services in the United States, 1995–1996," *Family Planning Perspectives* 30.1 (1998):

[89] Ibid.

[90] Ibid.

[91] U.S. Department of Commerce, Bureau of the Census, *Statistical Abstract of the United States 1998* (Washington, DC: GPO, 1998).

[92] U.S. Department of Health and Human Services, Centers for Disease

Control and Prevention, "Abortion Surveillance—United States, 1995," "Morbidity and Mortality Weekly Report," Vol. 47, No. SS–2.

[93] Alan Guttmacher Institute, "Facts in Brief: Induced Abortion," 1998.

[94] Ibid.

[95] Aida Torres and Jacqueline Darroch Forrest, "Why Do Women Have Abortions?" *Family Planning Perspectives,* July/August 1988.

[96] U.S. Department of Health and Human Services, Centers for Disease Control and Prevention, "Abortion Surveillance—United States, 1995," "Morbidity and Mortality Weekly Report," Vol. 47, No. SS–2.

[97] Alan Guttmacher Institute, "Facts in Brief: Induced Abortion," 1998.

[98] Alan Guttmacher Institute, "Abortion Incidence and Services in the United States, 1995–1996," *Family Planning Perspectives* 30.1 (1998).

[99] Thomas R. Eng and William T. Butler, eds., *The Hidden Epidemic* (Washington: National Academy Press, 1997).

[100] Ibid.

[101] U.S. Department of Health and Human Services, Centers for Disease Control and Prevention, "HIV/AIDS Surveillance Report," Vol. 10, No. 1, Vol. 8, No. 2, and Vol. 6, No. 2.

[102] U.S. Department of Health and Human Services, Centers for Disease Control and Prevention, "Tracking the Hidden Epidemics: Trends in the STD Epidemics in the United States," 1998.

[103] Cheryl Wetzstein, "Researchers Raise Sex–Disease Estimate," *Washington Times,* December 3, 1998.

[104] Alan Guttmacher Institute, "Facts in Brief: Teen Sex and Pregnancy," 1998.

[105] Thomas R. Eng and William T. Butler, eds., *The Hidden Epidemic* (Washington: National Academy Press, 1997).

CHAPTER THREE

Education

PERFORMANCE:
Third International Mathematics and Science Study (TIMSS)

Mathematics

- In the most recent (1996) international comparison in mathematics achievement, American fourth graders ranked twelfth out of twenty-six nations; eighth graders ranked twenty-eighth out of forty-one nations; and twelfth graders ranked nineteenth out of twenty-one nations.*

U.S. vs. International Performance on TIMSS: Mathematics

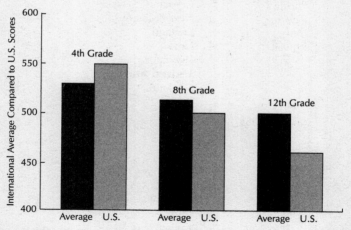

* Some countries that finished among the highest in fourth- and eighth-grade tests in math or science—including Singapore, Korea, Japan, and Hong Kong—did not take the twelfth-grade test.

TIMSS Mathematics Scores, 1996

Rank	Fourth Grade	Eighth Grade	Twelfth Grade
1	Singapore	Singapore	Netherlands
2	Korea	Korea	Sweden
3	Japan	Japan	Denmark
4	Hong Kong	Hong Kong	Switzerland
5	Netherlands	Belgium—Flemish	Iceland
6	Czech Republic	Czech Republic	Norway
7	Austria	Slovak Republic	France
8	Slovenia	Switzerland	New Zealand
9	Ireland	Netherlands	Australia
10	Hungary	Slovenia	Canada
11	Australia	Bulgaria	Austria
12	**United States**	Austria	Slovenia
13	Canada	France	Germany
14	Israel	Hungary	Hungary
15	Latvia	Russia	Italy
16	Scotland	Australia	Russia
17	England	Ireland	Lithuania
18	Cyprus	Canada	Czech Republic
19	Norway	Belgium—French	**United States**
20	New Zealand	Sweden	Cyprus
21	Greece	Thailand	South Africa
22	Thailand	Israel	
23	Portugal	Germany	
24	Iceland	New Zealand	
25	Iran	England	
26	Kuwait	Norway	
27		Denmark	
28		**United States**	
29		Scotland	
30		Latvia	
31		Spain	
32		Iceland	
33		Greece	
34		Romania	
35		Lithuania	
36		Cyprus	
37		Portugal	
38		Iran	
39		Kuwait	
40		Colombia	
41		South Africa	

Source: U.S. Department of Education

U.S. vs. International Performance on TIMSS: Mathematics

	Fourth Grade	Eighth Grade	Twelfth Grade
Average	529	513	500
U.S. score	545	500	461

Science

- In the most recent (1996) international comparison in science achievement, American fourth graders ranked third out of twenty-six nations; eighth graders ranked seventeenth out of forty-one nations; and twelfth graders ranked sixteenth out of twenty-one nations.

U.S. vs. International Performance on TIMSS: Science

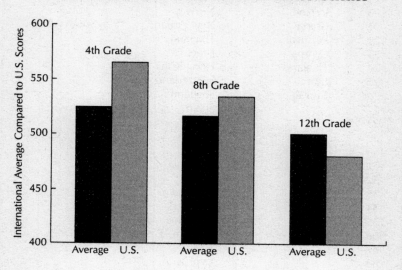

TIMSS Science Scores, 1996

Rank	Fourth Grade	Eighth Grade	Twelfth Grade
1	Korea	Singapore	Sweden
2	Japan	Czech Republic	Netherlands
3	**United States**	Japan	Iceland
4	Austria	Korea	Norway
5	Australia	Bulgaria	Canada
6	Netherlands	Netherlands	New Zealand
7	Czech Republic	Slovenia	Australia
8	England	Austria	Switzerland
9	Canada	Hungary	Austria
10	Singapore	England	Slovenia
11	Slovenia	Belgium—Flemish	Denmark
12	Ireland	Australia	Germany
13	Scotland	Slovak Republic	France
14	Hong Kong	Russia	Czech Republic
15	Hungary	Ireland	Russia
16	New Zealand	Sweden	**United States**
17	Norway	**United States**	Italy
18	Latvia	Germany	Hungary
19	Israel	Canada	Lithuania
20	Iceland	Norway	Cyprus
21	Greece	New Zealand	South Africa
22	Portugal	Thailand	
23	Cyprus	Israel	
24	Thailand	Hong Kong	
25	Iran	Switzerland	
26	Kuwait	Scotland	
27		Spain	
28		France	
29		Greece	
30		Iceland	
31		Romania	
32		Latvia	
33		Portugal	
34		Denmark	
35		Lithuania	
36		Belgium—French	
37		Iran	
38		Cyprus	
39		Kuwait	
40		Colombia	
41		South Africa	

Source: U.S. Department of Education

U.S. vs. International Performance on TIMSS: Science

	Fourth Grade	Eighth Grade	Twelfth Grade
Average	524	516	500
U.S. score	565	534	480

Advanced Physics

- Our advanced physics students ranked last among all nations taking the test.

**TIMSS Advanced Physics
Scores, 1996**

Rank	Twelfth Graders
1	Norway
2	Sweden
3	Russia
4	Denmark
5	Slovenia
6	Germany
7	Australia
8	Cyprus
9	Latvia
10	Switzerland
11	Greece
12	Canada
13	France
14	Czech Republic
15	Austria
16	**United States**

Source: U.S. Department of Education

Advanced Mathematics

- Our advanced mathematics students ranked fifteenth out of sixteen nations taking the test.

**TIMSS Advanced Mathematics
Scores, 1996**

Rank	Twelfth Graders
1	France
2	Russia
3	Switzerland
4	Australia
5	Denmark
6	Cyprus
7	Lithuania
8	Greece
9	Sweden
10	Canada
11	Slovenia
12	Italy
13	Czech Republic
14	Germany
15	**United States**
16	Austria

Source: U.S. Department of Education

PERFORMANCE:
National Assessment of Educational Progress (NAEP)

- *During the 1990s, student scores on the National Assessment of Educational Progress tests increased very slightly (although 17-year-old reading and eleventh-grade writing actually decreased slightly). Since the 1970s, scores have increased slightly on nine tests but decreased slightly on three (17-year-old science and eighth- and eleventh-grade writing).*

Average Reading Scale Scores

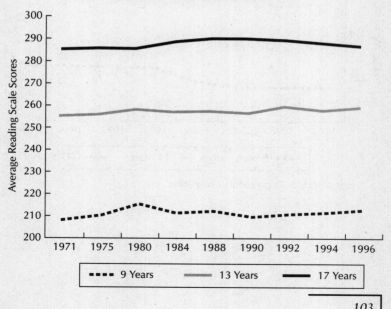

Average Reading Scale Scores

Age	1971	1975	1980	1984	1988	1990	1992	1994	1996
9	207.6	210.0	215.0	210.9	211.8	209.2	210.5	211.0	212.4
13	255.2	255.9	258.5	257.1	257.5	256.8	259.8	257.9	259.1
17	285.2	285.6	285.5	288.8	290.1	290.2	289.7	288.1	286.9

Source: U.S. Department of Education

Average Mathematics Scale Scores

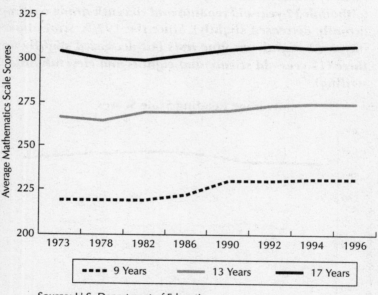

Source: U.S. Department of Education

Average Mathematics Scale Scores

Age	1973	1978	1982	1986	1990	1992	1994	1996
9	219	219	219	222	230	230	231	231
13	266	264	269	269	270	273	274	274
17	304	300	299	302	305	307	306	307

Source: U.S. Department of Education

Average Science Scale Scores

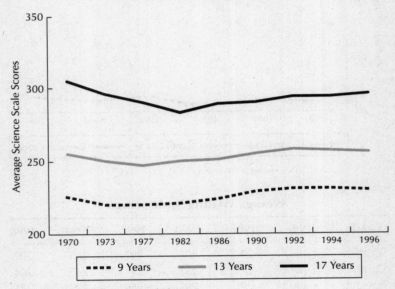

Source: U.S. Department of Education

Average Science Scale Scores

Age	1970	1973	1977	1982	1986	1990	1992	1994	1996
9	225	220	220	221	224	229	231	231	230
13	255	250	247	250	251	255	258	257	256
17	305	296	290	283	289	290	294	294	296

Source: U.S. Department of Education

Average Writing Scale Scores

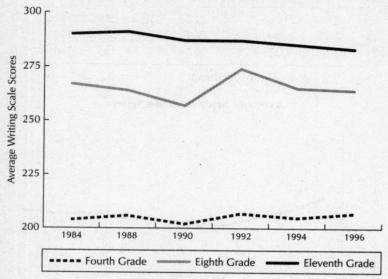

Source: U.S. Department of Education

Average Writing Scale Scores

Grade	1984	1988	1990	1992	1994	1996
Fourth	204	206	202	207	205	207
Eighth	267	264	257	274	265	264
Eleventh	290	291	287	287	285	283

Source: U.S. Department of Education

The States: 1996 NAEP Science Scores

• In 1996, Maine had the highest average science scale score for students in grade eight. Ten states did not participate.[1]

States Performing Above the National Average for Science Scale Scores in Grade Eight

State	Average Score
Maine	163
North Dakota	162
Montana	162
Wisconsin	160
Minnesota	159
Iowa	158
Wyoming	158
Nebraska	157
Vermont	157
Massachusetts	157
Utah	156
Connecticut	155
Oregon	155
Colorado	155
Michigan	153
Indiana	153
Alaska	153

States Performing at or Around the National Average

Missouri	151
Washington	150
Virginia	149
Rhode Island	149
U.S. national average	**148**

(continued next page)

States Performing at or Around
the National Average

Kentucky	147
West Virginia	147
North Carolina	147
New York	146
Maryland	145
Texas	145
Arizona	145

States Performing Below
the National Average

Arkansas	144
Tennessee	143
Florida	142
Georgia	142
Delaware	142
New Mexico	141
Alabama	139
South Carolina	139
California	138
Hawaii	135
Mississippi	133
Louisiana	132
District of Columbia	113

States Not Participating

Idaho
Illinois
Kansas
New Hampshire

(continued next page)

States Not Participating

New Jersey
Nevada
Ohio
Oklahoma
Pennsylvania
South Dakota

PERFORMANCE: SCHOLASTIC ASSESSMENT TEST (SAT)

- *Between 1990 and 1998, there was a 16-point increase in average SAT scores. But between 1960 and 1998, there was a 59-point decrease.**

Average SAT Scores: Total, Verbal, and Mathematical on Old and New Scales

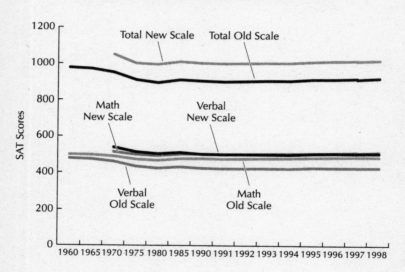

* In 1996, the College Board began reporting "recentered" SAT scores, which led to significantly higher scores. Therefore, to compare today's SAT scores with earlier scores, one or the other must be converted using information and conversion charts provided by the College Board. The chart and table of aver-

Average SAT Scores: Total, Verbal, and Mathematical
on Old and New Scales

Year	Total—Old Scale	Verbal—Old Scale	Math—Old Scale	Total—New Scale	Verbal—New Scale	Math—New Scale
1960	975	477	498	NA	NA	NA
1965	969	473	496	NA	NA	NA
1970	948	460	488	1049	537	512
1975	906	434	472	1000	512	498
1980	890	424	466	994	502	492
1985	906	431	475	1009	509	500
1990	900	424	476	1001	500	501
1991	896	422	474	999	499	500
1992	899	423	476	1001	500	501
1993	902	424	478	1003	500	503
1994	902	423	479	1003	499	504
1995	910	428	482	1010	504	506
1996	911	427	484	1014	506	508
1997	915	428	487	1016	505	511
1998	916	428	488	1017	505	512

Source: College Board, Thomas B. Fordham Foundation

Factual Overview: Student Achievement

- Average verbal scores on the SAT decreased 49 points between 1960 and 1998, while math scores decreased 10 points.[2]

---

age SAT scores include scores on both the new and the old scales (source: Thomas B. Fordham Foundation). Readers should be aware that the SAT is taken predominantly by students intending to attend college and hence involves an unrepresentative sample. It is also important to note that in some states (particularly in the Midwest and West) most college-bound students take the ACT in place of the SAT.

- Average SAT scores were at their highest level (980) in 1963. Between 1963 and 1980, when they were at their lowest level, scores dropped 90 points.[3]
- Between 1985–86 and 1995–96, the number of bachelor's degrees awarded to men increased 8 percent (from 485,923 to 522,454), while those awarded to women increased 28 percent (from 501,900 to 642,338).[4]
- In 1998, 38 percent of fourth graders, 26 percent of eighth graders, and 23 percent of twelfth graders scored below basic levels in reading (that is, they lack even partial mastery of the knowledge and skills appropriate to their grade). For fourth graders, this means that they cannot "demonstrate an understanding of the overall meaning of what they read." For eighth graders, this means they cannot "demonstrate a literal understanding of what they read and be able to make some interpretation." For twelfth graders, this means they cannot "demonstrate an overall understanding and make some interpretations of the text.... They [cannot] identify elements of an author's style."[5]
- Since 1983, more than 10 million Americans have reached the twelfth grade without having learned to read at a basic level. More than 20 million have reached their senior year unable to do basic math. Almost 25 million have reached the twelfth grade without knowing the essentials of U.S. history.[6]
- In the fourth grade, 77 percent of children in urban high-poverty areas are reading below the basic level on the NAEP tests.[7]
- Average black and Hispanic 17–year–olds have NAEP scores in math, science, reading, and writing that are equivalent to the average score of white 13–year–olds.[8]
- A recent study of home–schooled children found that they score well above the national median on standardized tests and often study at a level above most students in their grade.[9]

SPENDING

- *Between 1990 and 1998, per pupil public school expenditures increased (in constant dollars) 5 percent. Between 1960 and 1998, per pupil expenditures increased (in constant dollars) 187 percent.*[10]

Per Pupil Expenditures on Public Elementary and Secondary Schools

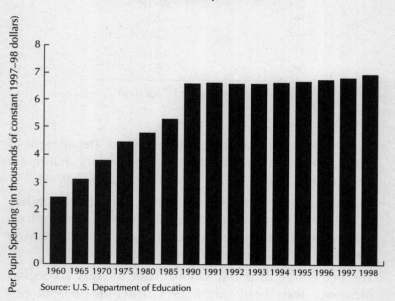

Source: U.S. Department of Education

Per Pupil Expenditures on Public Elementary and Secondary Schools

Year	Spending (constant 1997–98 dollars)
1960	2,422
1965	3,077
1970	3,764
1975	4,444
1980	4,770
1985	5,285
1990	6,591
1991	6,626
1992	6,587
1993	6,587
1994	6,633
1995	6,676
1996	6,745
1997	6,814
1998	6,943

Source: U.S. Department of Education

Factual Overview: School Spending

- According to preliminary estimates by the Department of Education, public elementary and secondary education expenditures rose to a high of $324.3 billion in 1997–98.[11]

- The total amount spent on public elementary and secondary education in 1995–96 was $293.6 billion. Of this amount, 6.6 percent came from the federal government, 47.5 percent from the states, and 45.9 percent from local governments.[12]

- The percentage of public schools with Internet access has increased dramatically since 1994. Three-quarters of elementary schools are connected to the Internet (an increase of 150 percent) and almost 90 percent of secondary schools (an increase of 82 percent).[13]

• While the level of spending per pupil has increased by more than 70 percent (in constant dollars) since the 1970s, student achievement, as measured by the National Assessment of Educational Progress, has stayed relatively level.[14]

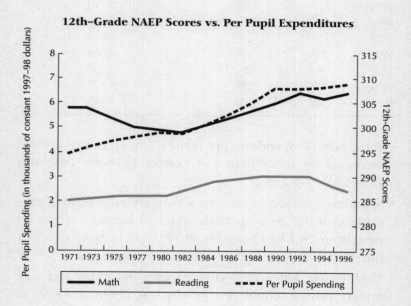

12th–Grade NAEP Scores vs. Per Pupil Expenditures

Twelfth–Grade NAEP Scores vs. Per Pupil Expenditures

Year	Math	Reading	Per Pupil Spending (in constant 1997–98 dollars)
1971		285	3,950
1973	304		4,219
1975		286	4,444
1977	300		4,612
1980		286	4,770
1982	299		4,734
1984		289	5,110
1986	302		5,536
1988		290	6,018
1990	305	290	6,591
1992	307	290	6,587
1994	306	288	6,633
1996	307	287	6,745

- Total school spending per capita (in constant dollars) increased by more than 140 percent between 1960 and 1995–96.[15]

- Spending on elementary and secondary schools as a percentage of the gross domestic product increased from 3.6 percent in 1961 to 4.3 percent in 1997—an increase of about one–fifth.[16]

- The average full tuition charged by elementary and secondary private schools in 1993–94 was $3,116. Students at Catholic schools paid an average of $2,178, and students at nonsectarian private schools paid $6,631.[17]

- Measured in constant 1997–98 dollars, the average annual salary of teachers in public elementary and secondary schools has increased from $27,496 in 1960 to $39,385 in 1998—an increase of 43 percent.[18]

• The average teaching work year lasts 180 days, three-quarters of the 240–day year worked by the typical American with a full–time job. Compensated at the same daily rate for a forty–eight–week year, the average public school teacher would have earned $52,513 in 1998.[19]

The States: Per Pupil Expenditures and Achievement

• In 1996, New Jersey had the highest rate of per pupil expenditures; however, it did not participate in the NAEP tests. The District of Columbia had the second highest rate of per pupil expenditures and ranked last in NAEP's eighth–grade math test. On the other hand, Iowa, Maine, North Dakota, and Minnesota had the highest NAEP scores, but ranked twenty–eighth, eighteenth, forty–fourth, and twenty–seventh, respectively, in terms of per pupil expenditures.[20] (Note: Only forty states–plus the District of Columbia–participated in the test.)

States by Per Pupil Expenditures, 1996

State	Expenditure	Rank in NAEP's 1996 Eighth–Grade Math Test
New Jersey	$10,241	NA
District of Columbia	$9,123	41
New York	$8,564	20
Connecticut	$8,469	8
Alaska	$8,253	10
Massachusetts	$7,587	10
Rhode Island	$7,263	24
Pennsylvania	$7,204	NA
Delaware	$7,086	27
Vermont	$6,982	9

(continued next page)

State	Expenditure	Rank in NAEP's 1996 Eighth–Grade Math Test
New Mexico	$6,887	33
Michigan	$6,650	12
Maryland	$6,503	20
Wisconsin	$6,467	5
Illinois	$6,398	NA
New Hampshire	$6,320	NA
Georgia	$6,243	33
Maine	$6,169	1
Virginia	$6,088	20
Oregon	$6,047	14
Wyoming	$6,024	18
Nebraska	$6,016	5
West Virginia	$6,015	29
Ohio	$5,968	NA
Indiana	$5,947	14
Washington	$5,929	14
Minnesota	$5,826	1
Iowa	$5,699	1
Kentucky	$5,655	27
Kansas	$5,505	NA
Texas	$5,501	20
California	$5,469	31
Florida	$5,365	30
Colorado	$5,337	14
Montana	$5,337	5
Hawaii	$5,210	33
North Carolina	$5,190	25
Tennessee	$5,127	31
Nevada	$5,016	NA
Missouri	$4,988	19
South Carolina	$4,928	37
South Dakota	$4,924	NA

(continued next page)

State	Expenditure	Rank in NAEP's 1996 Eighth–Grade Math Test
Oklahoma	$4,895	NA
North Dakota	$4,886	1
Alabama	$4,669	38
Arizona	$4,495	25
Louisiana	$4,490	39
Idaho	$4,445	NA
Mississippi	$4,164	40
Utah	$3,385	12
Arkansas	$3,378	33

- Of the five states that had the highest increase in per pupil expenditures between 1978 and 1998, three were below the national average increase on SAT scores and none was in the top ten.[21]

Increase in Per Pupil Expenditures and SAT Scores, 1978–98

State	Increase in per Pupil Expenditures	Change in SAT Scores	Rank by Score Change
Georgia	108.2%	4.5%	11
West Virginia	101.9	−3.0	47
New Hampshire	97.8	0.9	31
New Jersey	94.5	3.0	17
New Mexico	94.0	0.0	36

- Of the five states that had the highest increase in SAT scores between 1978 and 1998, none was in the top ten states measured by per pupil expenditures.[22]

Increase in SAT Scores and Per Pupil Expenditures, 1978–98

State	Increase in SAT Scores	Increase in per Pupil Expenditures	Rank by Expenditure Increase
Florida	13.1%	44.7%	35
Alabama	11.2	54.3	21
District of Columbia	8.9	78.4	12
Missouri	6.8	55.3	20
Illinois	6.8	41.5	37

PUBLIC SCHOOLS

- *Between 1990 and 1996, the percentage of full-time school staff who are teachers decreased 2.4 percent. Between 1960 and 1996, the percentage decreased almost 20 percent.*[25]

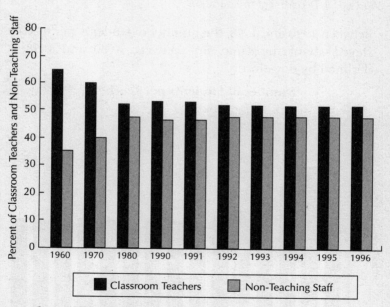

Composition of Full–Time School Staff (Percent)

Source: U.S. Department of Education

Composition of Full–Time School Staff (Percent)

Year	Classroom Teachers	Nonteaching Staff
1960	64.8	35.2
1970	60.0	40.0
1980	52.4	47.6
1990	53.4	46.6
1991	53.3	46.7
1992	52.2	47.8
1993	52.1	47.9
1994	52.0	48.0
1995	52.0	48.0
1996	52.1	47.9

Source: U.S. Department of Education

- Between 1990 and 1998, the number of students per teacher stayed about the same. But between 1960 and 1998, it declined by one–third.[24]

Number of Students per Teacher

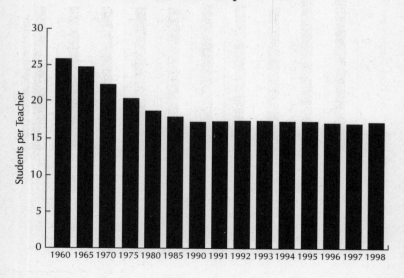

Number of Students per Teacher

Year	Students per Teacher
1960	25.8
1965	24.7
1970	22.3
1975	20.4
1980	18.7
1985	17.9
1990	17.2
1991	17.3
1992	17.4
1993	17.4
1994	17.3
1995	17.3
1996	17.1
1997	17.0
1998	17.2

Factual Overview: Public School Staff

- The number of guidance counselors in public elementary and secondary schools increased more than 500 percent between 1960 and 1998. There was an almost tenfold increase in teacher's aides. The number of support staff increased almost 170 percent. Over the same time span, the number of teachers increased 97 percent.[25]

- The pupil–teacher ratio in private elementary and secondary schools is fifteen to one; in public schools, it is seventeen to one.[26]

Factual Overview: School Enrollment and Dropouts

- In 1997, more than one-fourth of the American population was enrolled in school. Enrollment at the elementary and secondary levels was 48.2 million.[27]

- In 1996, private school enrollment at the elementary and secondary level was 5.8 million.[28]
- In 1996–97, the 433 charter schools then in existence educated 110,122 students.[29]
- The percentage of 3-to-5-year-olds enrolled in preprimary school programs rose from 27.1 in 1965 to 64.8 in 1997.[30]
- The number of children schooled at home increased from 10,000 in 1980 to approximately 1 million in 1996.[31]
- The percentage of high school dropouts among persons 16 to 24 decreased by almost 60 percent between 1960 and 1997.[32]

Percent of High School Dropouts Among Persons 16 to 24

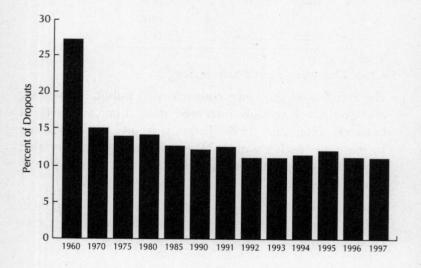

Percent of High School Dropouts Among Persons 16 to 24

Year	Total	White	Black	Hispanic
1960	27.2	NA	NA	NA
1965	NA	NA	NA	NA
1970	15.0	13.2	27.9	NA
1975	13.9	11.4	22.9	29.2
1980	14.1	11.4	19.1	35.2
1985	12.6	10.4	15.2	27.6
1990	12.1	9.0	13.2	32.4
1991	12.5	8.9	13.6	35.3
1992	11.0	7.7	13.7	29.4
1993	11.0	7.9	13.6	27.5
1994	11.4	7.7	12.6	30.0
1995	12.0	8.6	12.1	30.0
1996	11.1	7.3	13.0	29.4
1997	11.0	7.6	13.4	25.3

- In 1996, the median income of men 25 years of age and older with a high school diploma or an equivalency degree was $24,814, while the median income for those without a high school diploma was $16,058. The numbers for women were $12,702 and $8,544, respectively.[33]

- In 1997, 82.1 percent of Americans aged 25 and over had completed high school. This includes 84.9 percent of Asians, 83 percent of whites, 74.9 percent of blacks, and 54.7 percent of Hispanics.[34]

The States: Graduation Levels

- In 1997, Alaska had the highest percentage of Americans over age 25 who had graduated from high school or earned an equivalency degree (92.1 percent). Kentucky had the lowest percentage (75.4).[35]

Highest	Lowest
Alaska: 92.1	Kentucky: 75.4
Wyoming: 91.3	Louisiana: 75.7
Utah: 89.5	Tennessee: 76.1
Washington: 88.8	Arkansas: 76.9
Montana: 88.6	South Carolina: 77.3
	West Virginia: 77.3

NOTES

[1] U.S. Department of Education, National Center for Education Statistics, "NAEP 1996 Science Report Card."

[2] College Board, Thomas B. Fordham Foundation.

[3] Ibid.

[4] U.S. Department of Education, National Center for Education Statistics, *Digest of Education Statistics 1998* (Washington, DC: GPO, 1999).

[5] U.S. Department of Education, National Center for Education Statistics, "1998 Reading Report Card for the Nation and the States."

[6] *A Nation Still at Risk: An Education Manifesto,* April 1998.

[7] *Quality Counts '98: The Urban Challenge* (Washington, DC: Editorial Projects in Education, January 8, 1998).

[8] Lawrence Stedman, "An Assessment of the Contemporary Debate over U.S. Achievement," in *Brookings Papers on Education Policy 1998* (Washington, DC: The Brookings Institution, 1998).

[9] Jay Mathews, "A Home Run for Home Schooling," *Washington Post,* March 24, 1999.

[10] U.S. Department of Education, National Center for Education Statistics, *Digest of Education Statistics 1998* (Washington, DC: GPO, 1999).

[11] Ibid.

[12] Ibid.

[13] U.S. Department of Commerce, Census Bureau, *Statistical Abstract of the United States 1998* (Washington, DC: GPO, 1998).

[14] U.S. Department of Education, National Center for Education Statistics, *Digest of Education Statistics 1998* (Washington, DC: GPO, 1999).

[15] Ibid.

[16] Ibid.

[17] Ibid.

[18] Ibid.

[19] Ibid.

[20] American Legislative Exchange Council, "Report Card on American Education: A State–by–State Analysis," December 1998.

[21] Ibid.

[22] Ibid.

[23] U.S. Department of Education, National Center for Education Statistics, *Digest of Education Statistics 1998* (Washington, DC: GPO, 1999).

[24] Ibid.

[25] Ibid.

[26] Ibid.

[27] U.S. Department of Commerce, Census Bureau, "School Enrollment— Social and Economic Characteristics of Students," July 1999.

[28] U.S. Department of Education, National Center for Education Statistics, *Digest of Education Statistics 1998* (Washington, DC: GPO, 1999).

[29] American Legislative Exchange Council, "Report Card on American Education: A State–by–State Analysis," December 1998.

[30] U.S. Department of Education, National Center for Education Statistics, *Digest of Education Statistics 1998* (Washington, DC: GPO, 1999).

[31] Dana Mack, *The Assault on Parenthood* (New York: Simon & Schuster, 1997).

[32] U.S. Department of Education, National Center for Education Statistics, *Digest of Education Statistics 1998* (Washington, DC: GPO, 1999).

[33] Ibid.

[34] U.S. Department of Commerce, Census Bureau, *Statistical Abstract of the United States 1998* (Washington, DC: GPO, 1998).

[35] Ibid.

CHAPTER FOUR

Youth Behavior

OUT-OF-WEDLOCK TEENAGE BIRTHS

- *Between 1990 and 1996, the percentage of all teenage mothers who are unmarried has increased 12 percent. Between 1960 and 1996, the percentage increased more than 400 percent.*

Teenage Out-of-Wedlock Births

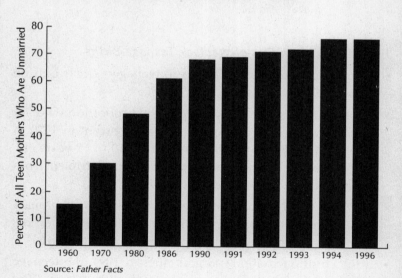

Source: *Father Facts*

Teenage Out–of–Wedlock Births

Year	Percentage of All Teen Mothers Who Are Unmarried
1960	15
1970	30
1980	48
1986	61
1990	68
1991	69
1992	71
1993	72
1994	76
1995	NA
1996	76

Source: *Father Facts*

Factual Overview: Out-of-Wedlock Teenage Births

- Seventy–six percent of all births to teenagers occur outside of marriage.[1]

- Among mothers 15 to 17 years old, the proportion who are unmarried more than doubled, from 43 percent in 1970 to 87 percent in 1997. Similarly, for mothers 18 to 19 years old, the proportion who are unmarried more than tripled, from 22 percent in 1970 to 72 percent in 1997.[2]

- In 1994, 67 percent of white teenage mothers were unmarried; 70 percent of Hispanic teenage mothers were unmarried; and 96 percent of black teenage mothers were unmarried.[3]

- In fifteen of our nation's largest cities in 1995, the teenage out–of–wedlock birth ratio was greater than 90 percent.[4] The cities with the highest out–of–wedlock birth ratio for girls under 20 are Baltimore and Pittsburgh.[5]

**Out–of–Wedlock Births as Percentage of
All Births to Girls under 20, 1995**

City	Percent
Baltimore	96.5
Pittsburgh	96.5
New Orleans	96.4
St. Louis	96.1
Philadelphia	95.8
Washington, D.C.	95.6
Detroit	95.5
Cincinnati	94.6
Buffalo	93.4
Cleveland	93.3

- As recently as 1975, more than half of all births to unmarried women were to teenagers; by 1997, the proportion had dropped to less than a third.[6]

- More than half of women who gave birth as teenagers had total family incomes below 50 percent of the poverty line in 1992.[7]

- About 80 percent of the children born to unmarried teenagers who dropped out of high school are poor. But only 8 percent of the children born to married high school graduates aged 20 or older are poor.[8]

Factual Overview: Teenage Fertility and Out-of-Wedlock Birth Rates

- Since 1990, the teenage fertility rate has dropped nearly 13 percent, while the teenage out–of–wedlock birth rate has decreased less than 1 percent. Between 1970 and 1997, the teenage fertility rate decreased 23.4 percent, while the teenage out–of–wedlock birth rate increased 88 percent.[9]

Teenage Fertility and Out-of-Wedlock Birth Rate

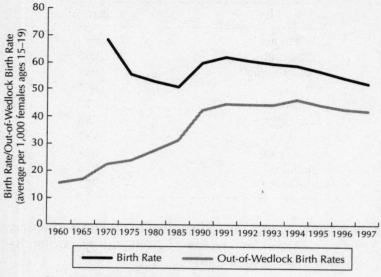

Source: U.S. Department of Health and Human Services

Teenage Fertility and Out-of-Wedlock Birth Rate

Year	Birth Rate (per 1,000 girls aged 15–19)	Out-of-Wedlock Birth Rate (average number of births per 1,000 unmarried girls aged 15–19)
1960	NA	15.3
1965	NA	16.7
1970	68.3	22.4
1975	55.6	23.9
1980	53.0	27.6
1985	51.0	31.4
1990	59.9	42.5
1991	62.1	44.8

(continued next page)

Year	Birth Rate (per 1,000 girls aged 15–19)	Out-of-Wedlock Birth Rate (average number of births per 1,000 unmarried girls aged 15–19)
1992	60.7	44.6
1993	59.6	44.5
1994	58.9	46.4
1995	56.8	44.4
1996	54.4	42.9
1997	52.3	42.2

The States: Out-of-Wedlock Teenage Births

• In every state in America, a majority of births to teenagers are out of wedlock.[10]

Out-of-Wedlock Teenage Births, 1996

State	Percent of Mothers Aged 15–19 Who Are Unmarried
District of Columbia	97
Rhode Island	92
Massachusetts	90
Maryland	90
New Jersey	89
Pennsylvania	89
Delaware	88
Connecticut	88
New York	88
New Hampshire	88
Michigan	87
Minnesota	87
Vermont	85
Illinois	84

(continued next page)

State	Percent of Mothers Aged 15–19 Who Are Unmarried
Ohio	84
Wisconsin	84
Louisiana	83
Maine	82
Hawaii	82
South Dakota	82
Nebraska	81
Iowa	81
Mississippi	80
South Carolina	80
Arizona	80
North Dakota	80
Indiana	80
Florida	79
New Mexico	79
Missouri	78
Montana	78
Virginia	78
Alaska	77
Nevada	77
Georgia	76
Washington	75
North Carolina	75
Kansas	74
Oregon	74
Colorado	72
Tennessee	70
Wyoming	70
Alabama	70
West Virginia	67
Arkansas	67
Texas	66

(continued next page)

State	Percent of Mothers Aged 15–19 Who Are Unmarried
Oklahoma	66
Kentucky	65
California	62
Idaho	60
Utah	58

Factual Overview: Teenage Sexual Activity

- In 1970, 29 percent of girls aged 15 to 19 had had sexual intercourse. In 1995, 50 percent had.[11]

Percent of Girls Aged 15–19 Who Have Had Sexual Intercourse

Year	Percent
1970	29
1975	36
1982	47
1988	53
1990	55
1995	50

- In 1997, 16 percent of high school students had had sexual intercourse with four or more people during their lives.[12]

- Among teenage mothers, the younger the girl, the wider the age gap between her and the male; in other words, young female mothers are not normally impregnated by men as young as they are. In fact, there is an average age gap of four years between mothers aged 15 to 17 and their partners.[13]

- In 1991, almost 70 percent of babies born to teenage girls were fathered by men 20 years of age or older.[14] About one in five births to unmarried teenagers is caused by men five or more years older than the mother.[15]

- One out of five girls who report having intercourse before age 15 says it was involuntary.[16]

- Among women born between 1951 and 1955, 23 percent were married to their partner at the time of first sexual intercourse. Among women born between 1971 and 1975, 2 percent were married to their partner at the time of first sexual intercourse.[17]

- During first-time sexual intercourse, the percentage of teenagers using contraception rose from 48 percent to 65 percent during the 1980s and then to 78 percent in 1998.[18]

- The percentage of high school senior girls who think "having a child without being married is experimenting with a worthwhile lifestyle or [is] not affecting anyone else" increased from 33 percent in 1976–1980 to 53 percent in 1991–1995.[19]

- Among college freshmen, in 1998, 40 percent believed that "if two people really like each other, it's all right for them to have sex even if they've known each other for a very short time." That was the lowest percentage ever recorded since the survey began in 1974. Fifty-four percent of male freshmen and 28 percent of female freshmen agreed with the statement in 1998.[20]

Factual Overview: Teenagers and Sexually Transmitted Diseases

- By age 24, at least one in three sexually active people will have contracted a sexually transmitted disease.[21]

- About a quarter of all new cases of sexually transmitted diseases occur in teens; two-thirds of cases occur in people aged 15 to 24.[22]

- In 1997, roughly 3 million teenagers—about one in four who are sexually active—acquired a sexually transmitted disease.[23]
- Teenagers have higher rates of gonorrhea than do sexually active men and women aged 20 to 44.[24]

TEENAGE ABORTION

- *Between 1990 and 1996, the teenage abortion rate has decreased 28 percent. But between 1973 and 1996, the teenage abortion rate increased 27 percent.*

Teenage Abortion Rate

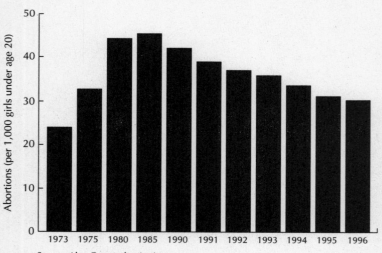

Source: Alan Guttmacher Institute

Legal Teenage Abortions

Year	Abortions (total number)	Abortion Rate (per 1,000 girls under age 20)
1973	243,530	23.9
1975	342,040	32.7
1980	460,120	44.3
1985	416,170	45.4
1990	363,550	42.1
1991	326,620	39.0
1992	308,190	37.0
1993	301,120	35.8
1994	288,530	33.6
1995	274,620	31.2
1996	274,300	30.3

Source: Alan Guttmacher Institute

Factual Overview: Teenage Abortion and Pregnancy

- Teenagers account for 20 percent of all abortions in the U.S. annually.[25]

- Teen pregnancy rates in the United States are twice as high as in England and Wales or Canada, and nine times as high as in the Netherlands or Japan.[26]

- Almost 1 million teenage girls in the United States get pregnant every year. Fifty-five percent of those pregnancies end in births; 31 percent result in abortions; and 14 percent result in miscarriages.[27]

- Seventy-eight percent of teenage pregnancies are unplanned.[28]

- Each year, 20 percent of girls aged 15 to 19 who have sexual intercourse will become pregnant.[29]

The States: Teenage Abortion

• In New Jersey, nearly six in ten teenage pregnancies ended in abortion in 1996. The proportion also exceeded 50 percent in New York, Massachusetts, and the District of Columbia.[30]

States with Highest Abortion Ratio
Among 15- to 19-Year-Old Girls, 1996

State	Abortions (per 100 teen pregnancies)
New Jersey	58
New York	56
District of Columbia	54
Massachusetts	53
Maryland	50
Connecticut	50

States with Lowest Abortion Ratio
Among 15- to 19-Year-Old Girls, 1996

State	Abortions (per 100 teen pregnancies)
Utah	15
Mississippi	17
Oklahoma	17
Kentucky	18
Arkansas	18

• Teenage abortion rates vary dramatically from state to state, ranging from 121 per 1,000 teens in the District of Columbia to 8 per 1,000 in Utah.[31]

States with Highest Teenage Abortion Rates, 1996

State	Abortion Rates (per 1,000 girls aged 15–19)
District of Columbia	·121
New York	53
Nevada	51
New Jersey	50
Maryland	46

States with Lowest Teenage Abortion Rates, 1996

State	Abortion Rate (per 1,000 girls aged 15–19)
Utah	8
North Dakota	10
South Dakota	10
West Virginia	11
Idaho	12
Iowa	12
Oklahoma	13

TEENAGE SUICIDE

- *Between 1990 and 1996, the teenage suicide rate decreased 13 percent. But between 1962 and 1996, the teenage suicide rate increased 155 percent.*

Teenage Suicide Rate

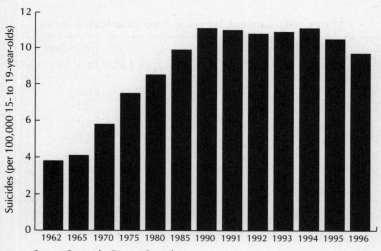

Source: Centers for Disease Control

Teenage Suicides

Year	Suicides (total number)	Suicide Rate (per 100,000 15- to 19-Year-Olds)
1962	556	3.8
1965	685	4.1
1970	1,123	5.8
1975	1,594	7.5
1980	1,797	8.5
1985	1,849	9.9
1990	1,979	11.1
1991	1,899	11.0
1992	1,847	10.8
1993	1,884	10.9
1994	1,948	11.1
1995	1,890	10.5
1996	1,817	9.7

Source: Centers for Disease Control

Factual Overview: Teenage Suicide and Depression

- Suicide is the third leading cause of death among persons aged 10 to 24. Motor vehicle accidents and homicide are the two leaders.[32]

- Once uncommon, suicides among black adolescents have increased sharply in recent years. Although white teenagers still have a higher rate of suicide, the gap between them is narrowing.[33]

- Of all Americans born in the mid-1970s, 12 to 15 percent of them have experienced at least one episode of serious depression.[34]

The States: Teenage Suicide

• Three states with below–average crime rates—North Dakota, South Dakota, and Montana—have the nation's highest teenage suicide rates.[35]

States with Highest Teenage Suicide Rates, 1996

State	Suicide Rate (per 100,000 15– to 19–year–olds)
Alaska	28.3
North Dakota	23.3
South Dakota	22.9
Arizona	17.8
Utah	17.8

States with Lowest Teenage Suicide Rates, 1996

State	Suicide Rate (per 100,000 15– to 19–year–olds)
New Jersey	3.6
Maryland	5.6
Ohio	5.7
Maine	5.7
New York	5.9

TEENAGE DRUG AND ALCOHOL ABUSE

- *Between 1990 and 1998, the percentage of high school seniors using illegal drugs has increased 13 percent. Overall, between 1975 and 1998, illegal drug use has decreased slightly.*

Lifetime Use of Any Illegal Drug

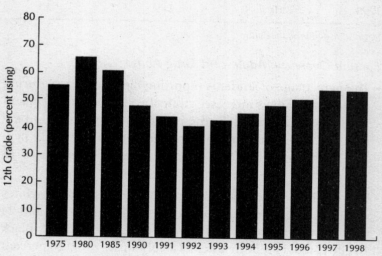

Source: *Monitoring the Future*

Lifetime Use of Any Illegal Drug

Year	Eighth Grade (percent using)	Tenth Grade (percent using)	Twelfth Grade (percent using)
1975	NA	NA	55.2
1980	NA	NA	65.4
1985	NA	NA	60.6
1990	NA	NA	47.9
1991	18.7	30.6	44.1
1992	20.6	29.8	40.7
1993	22.5	32.8	42.9
1994	25.7	37.4	45.6
1995	28.5	40.9	48.4
1996	31.2	45.4	50.8
1997	29.4	47.3	54.3
1998	29.0	44.9	54.1

Source: *Monitoring the Future*

Factual Overview: Adolescent Drug Abuse

• The percentage of students reporting illegal drug use during the last thirty days increased dramatically between 1992 and 1996. For twelfth graders, the proportion rose from 14 percent to 26 percent; for tenth graders, 11 percent to 23 percent; and for eighth graders, it rose from 7 percent to 15 percent.[36]

• Among high school seniors in 1997, 26 percent of whites reported illegal drug use, while 20 percent of blacks and 24 percent of Hispanics did. Similarly, 13 percent of black twelfth graders reported heavy alcohol use, while 28 percent of Hispanics and 35 percent of whites did.[37]

Lifetime Drug Use Among High School Seniors
(percent who have ever used)[38]

Year	Alcohol	Hallucinogen	Cocaine	Marijuana
1975	90.4	16.3	9.0	47.3
1980	93.2	13.3	15.7	60.3
1985	92.2	10.3	17.3	54.2
1990	89.5	9.4	9.4	40.7
1991	88.0	9.6	7.8	36.7
1992	87.5	9.2	6.1	32.6
1993	87.0	10.9	6.1	35.3
1994	80.4	11.4	5.9	38.2
1995	80.7	12.7	6.0	41.7
1996	79.2	14.0	7.1	44.9
1997	81.7	15.1	8.7	49.6
1998	81.4	14.1	9.3	49.1

- The percentage of high school seniors reporting *daily* usage of marijuana in 1998 was 5.6, a 180 percent increase since 1991.[39]

Daily Use of Marijuana
Among High School Seniors

Year	Percent Using
1991	2.0
1992	1.9
1993	2.4
1994	3.6
1995	4.6
1996	4.9
1997	5.8
1998	5.6

• The percentage of eighth graders who report having used marijuana during the past 30 days has more than tripled since 1991.[40]

Eighth–Grade Marijuana Use

Year	Past Thirty Days (percent using)	Past Year (percent using)	Lifetime (percent using)
1991	3.2	6.2	10.2
1992	3.7	7.2	11.2
1993	5.1	9.2	12.6
1994	7.8	13.0	16.7
1995	9.1	15.8	19.9
1996	11.3	18.3	23.1
1997	10.2	17.7	22.6
1998	9.7	16.9	22.2

Factual Overview: Adolescent Alcohol Abuse

• In 1997, almost one in three twelfth graders, one in four tenth graders, and more than one in ten eighth graders had at least five drinks in a row in the previous two weeks.[41]

• Use of alcohol by high school seniors has decreased in all measures since 1975.[42]

Alcohol Use Among High School Seniors*

Year	Lifetime (percent using)	Past Year (percent using)	Past Month (percent using)	Daily Use During Past Thirty Days (percent)
1975	90.4	84.8	68.2	5.7
1980	93.2	87.9	72.0	6.0
1985	92.2	85.6	65.9	5.0

(continued next page)

Year	Lifetime (percent using)	Past Year (percent using)	Past Month (percent using)	Daily Use During Past Thirty Days (percent)
1990	89.5	80.6	57.1	3.7
1991	88.0	77.7	54.0	3.6
1992	87.5	76.8	51.3	3.4
1993	80.0	72.7	48.6	3.4
1994	80.4	73.0	50.1	2.9
1995	80.7	73.7	51.3	3.5
1996	79.2	72.5	50.8	3.7
1997	81.7	74.8	52.7	3.9
1998	81.4	74.3	52.0	3.9

*In 1993, the question was changed to specify that use of alcohol involved "more than a few sips."

Factual Overview: Ritalin[†]

- Nearly 4 million children are now taking Ritalin. This is more than twice the 1990 number.[43]

- Ninety percent of all Ritalin is consumed in the United States.[44]

- From 1990 to 1995, there were about two thousand thefts of Ritalin, putting Ritalin in the top ten most frequently reported pharmaceutical drugs diverted from licensed handlers.[45]

- According to a report released by the United Nations, 10 to 12 percent of all male schoolchildren in the United States take Ritalin.[46]

- In 1995, four hundred children between ages 10 and 14 were taken to hospital emergency rooms after episodes of Ritalin

[†] Ritalin is a legal stimulant drug prescribed to millions of American children, most of whom have been diagnosed with attention deficit disorder (ADD).

abuse. This is about the same number as for cocaine–abuse emergency–room visits each year for this age group.[47]

• Nearly 50 percent of doctors spend an hour or less with a child before making a diagnosis and prescribing medication.[48]

• Ritalin production has increased 700 percent since 1990.[49]

• Ritalin consumption increased 264 percent between 1990 and 1996.[50]

Ritalin Consumption

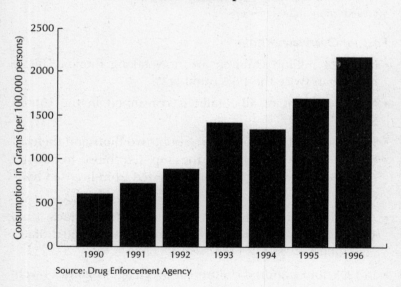

Source: Drug Enforcement Agency

Ritalin Consumption

Year	Consumption in Grams (per 100,000 persons)
1990	597.3
1991	716.0
1992	881.2
1993	1,413.8
1994	1,337.1
1995	1,693.5
1996	2,176.5

NOTES

[1] Alan Guttmacher Institute, "Facts in Brief: Teen Sex and Pregnancy," 1998.

[2] U.S. Department of Health and Human Services, Centers for Disease Control, and National Center for Health Statistics, "National Vital Statistics Report," Vol. 47, No. 12 (December, 1998).

[3] National Fatherhood Initiative, *Father Facts*, 1998.

[4] Wade F. Horn, "Did You Say 'Movement,' " *American Experiment Quarterly*, Winter 1998–99.

[5] U.S. Department of Health and Human Services, cited in National Fatherhood Initiative, *Father Facts*, 1998.

[6] U.S. Department of Health and Human Services, Centers for Disease Control, and National Center for Health Statistics, "National Vital Statistics Report," Vol. 47, No. 12 (December, 1998).

[7] U.S. General Accounting Office, cited in National Fatherhood Initiative, *Father Facts*, 1998.

[8] U.S. Department of Health and Human Services, "HHS Fact Sheet," April 1999.

[9] U.S. Department of Health and Human Services, Centers for Disease Control, and National Center for Health Statistics, "National Vital Statistics Report," Vol. 47, No. 18, April 1999.

[10] National Center for Health Statistics, *Monthly Vital Statistics Report*, cited in Annie E. Casey Foundation, "KIDS COUNT Special Report," rev. ed., 1998.

[11] "National Survey of Family Growth," 1995, cited in "America's Youth: Measuring the Risk," The Institute for Youth Development, 1998.

[12] U.S. Department of Health and Human Services, Centers for Disease Control, "Assessing Health Risk Behaviors Among Young People: Youth Risk Behavior Surveillance System," 1998.

[13] "How Old Are U.S. Fathers?" *Family Planning Perspectives,* cited in Michael Lynch, *Public Interest,* Summer 1998.

[14] National Center for Health Statistics, cited in National Fatherhood Initiative, *Father Facts,* 1998.

[15] Alan Guttmacher Institute, "Facts in Brief: Teen Sex and Pregnancy," 1998.

[16] National Center for Health Statistics, *Monthly Vital Statistics Report,* Vol. 46, No. 11, *www.cdc.gov/nchswww/datawh/statab/pubd/2319_21.htm.*

[17] U.S. Department of Health and Human Services, Vital and Health Statistics, "Fertility, Family Planning, and Women's Health," Series 23, No. 19, May 1997.

[18] Alan Guttmacher Institute, "Facts in Brief: Teen Sex and Pregnancy," 1998.

[19] David Popenoe and Barbara Dafoe Whitehead, "The State of Our Unions: The Social Health of Marriage in America" (New Brunswick, NJ: National Marriage Project, June 1999).

[20] L. J. Sax, A. W. Astin, W. S. Korn, K. M. Mahoney, "The American Freshman: National Norms for Fall 1998," Los Angeles: Higher Education Research Institute, UCLA.

[21] Henry J. Kaiser Family Foundation, "Sexually Transmitted Diseases in America: How Many Cases and at What Cost?" December 1998.

[22] Ibid.

[23] Ibid.

[24] Alan Guttmacher Institute, "Facts in Brief: Teen Sex and Pregnancy," 1998.

[25] Centers for Disease Control, "Abortion Surveillance—United States, 1995," Table 4.

[26] Alan Guttmacher Institute, "Facts in Brief: Teen Sex and Pregnancy," 1998.

[27] Ibid.

[28] Ibid.

[29] Ibid.

[30] Alan Guttmacher Institute, "Teenage Pregnancy: Overall Trends and State-by-State Information," April 1999.

[31] Ibid.

[32] U.S. Department of Health and Human Services, Centers for Disease Control, "Assessing Health Risk Behaviors Among Young People: Youth Risk Behavior Surveillance System," 1998.

[33] Ibid.

[34] Martin Seligman, professor of psychology at the University of Pennsylvania and president of the American Psychological Association, cited in William R. Mattox, Jr., "Bawling Alone," *Policy Review*, September/October 1998.

[35] Centers for Disease Control, unpublished data.

[36] Forum on Child and Family Statistics. "America's Children 1998," *http://www.childstats.gov/ac1998/behtxt.htm*.

[37] National Institute on Drug Abuse, *Monitoring the Future Study*, 1998.

[38] Ibid.

[39] Ibid.

[40] Ibid.

[41] Ibid.

[42] Ibid.

[43] Mary Eberstadt, "Why Ritalin Rules," *Policy Review*, April/May 1999.

[44] Lawrence H. Diller, *Running on Ritalin* (New York: Bantam), 1998.

[45] Drug Enforcement Agency, cited in Mary Eberstadt, "Why Ritalin Rules," *Policy Review*, April/May 1999.

[46] Ken Livingston, "Ritalin: Miracle Drug or Cop-Out?" *Public Interest*, Spring 1997.

[47] Mary Eberstadt, "Letters," *Policy Review*, June/July 1999.

[48] Ken Livingston, "Ritalin: Miracle Drug or Cop-Out?" *Public Interest*, Spring 1997.

[49] Lawrence H. Diller, *Running on Ritalin* (New York: Bantam, 1998).

[50] U.S. Department of Justice, Drug Enforcement Agency, unpublished data.

CHAPTER FIVE

Popular Culture and Religion

TELEVISION

- **In 1960, the average American household watched 5:06 hours of television a day. By 1997, the hours had increased to 7:12.**

Average Daily Television Viewing per Household

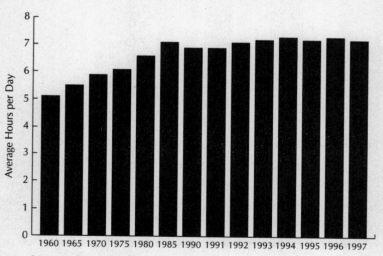

Source: Nielsen Media Research

Average Daily Television Viewing per Household

Year	Average Hours per Day
1960	5:06
1965	5:29
1970	5:56
1975	6:07
1980	6:36
1985	7:07
1990	6:55
1991	6:56
1992	7:04
1993	7:12
1994	7:16
1995	7:15
1996	7:17
1997	7:12

Source: Nielsen Media Research

Factual Overview: Television Viewing

- The average American watches more than four hours of television a day.[1]

- Ninety-eight percent of U.S. households have at least one television set.[2]

- Seventy-four percent of American households have two or more television sets; 40 percent have three or more.[3]

- In 1999, more 10-to-17-year-olds knew that *The Simpsons* television show featured Homer, Bart, and Maggie than knew the name of the Vice President of the United States (91 percent vs. 63 percent). In addition, more *parents* knew what television show featured Homer, Bart, and Maggie than knew the Vice President's name (84 percent vs. 80 percent).[4]

- Since 1970, the percentage of households with cable television has increased tenfold.[5]

U.S. Households with Cable Television

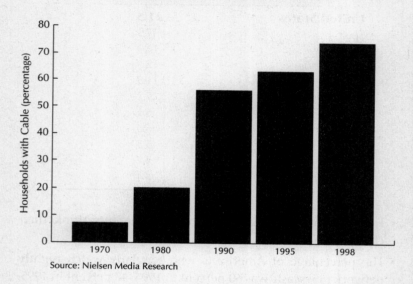

Source: Nielsen Media Research

- In 1996–97, 30.7 percent of U.S. homes used their television between 11:30 P.M. and 1:00 A.M.[6]

- Children between the ages of 2 and 17 spend, on average, more than three hours per day watching television and videotapes. They spend about one hour per day on schoolwork.[7]

- In 1999, 60 percent of adolescents aged 12 to 17 reported having a television set in their bedroom.[8]

- Twenty-one percent of American 9-year-olds watch more than five hours of television per weekday—the highest percentage in the developed world.[9]

Youth Television Watching

Country	Percent of 9–Year–Olds Who Watch More Than 5 Hours of Television per Weekday
United States	**21.3**
Spain	17.5
Canada	14.9
Netherlands	12.6
Ireland	11.8
Italy	9.2
Finland	6.1
Denmark	6.0
France	5.5
Sweden	4.7
Germany	4.4

- Fewer than one–quarter of American parents think their child watches too much television.[10]

- The percentage of Americans who regularly watch nightly network newscasts was 60 percent in 1993, 48 percent in 1995, 42 percent in 1996, and 38 percent in 1998. The proportion that never watches nightly network newscasts doubled during that period, from 9 percent in 1993 to 18 percent in 1998.[11]

Factual Overview: Television Content

- The total number of violent scenes on television (excluding news and other nonfiction programming) increased by 74 percent in three years—from 1,002 in 1992 to 1,738 in 1995—and reached an average of almost ten incidents of violence per channel per hour during the 1995–96 television season. Violence is most concentrated in cable movies and cartoon shows.[12]

- Television violence involving gunplay rose 334 percent from 1992 to 1995.[13]

- A sexual act or reference occurs every four minutes on average during prime-time television.[14]

- Of all prime-time drama and sitcom programs that depict or imply sex, less than 10 percent mention that sex entails risks and consequences.[15]

- Between January 1997 and November 1998—a period during which a television-ratings system was adopted—sexual content, foul language, and violent content rose by more than 30 percent on network television.[16]

- In 1999, out of 102 prime-time shows on ABC, NBC, CBS, Fox, and Warner Bros. Networks, only 15 included fathers as regular, central characters.[17]

- From 1993 to 1996, advertising in child-oriented media increased more than 50 percent to $1.5 billion.[18]

- Between 1993 and 1996, when the murder rate was dropping, there was a 721 percent increase in the number of minutes network-evening-news programs spent covering homicide. Even after excluding O. J. Simpson stories, murder news rose by 356 percent between 1993 and 1996.[19]

MOVIES

- ***In 1998, movie attendance in America was 1.48 billion— the highest level ever.***

Movie Attendance in America

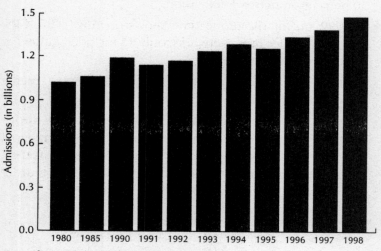

Source: Motion Picture Association of America

Movie Attendance in America

Year	Admissions (in billions)
1980	1.02
1985	1.06

(continued next page)

Year	Admissions (in billions)
1990	1.19
1991	1.14
1992	1.17
1993	1.24
1994	1.29
1995	1.26
1996	1.34
1997	1.39
1998	1.48

Source: Motion Picture Association of America

Factual Overview: Movies

- Since the beginning of the 1990s, U.S. box–office receipts have grown by nearly 40 percent to reach almost $7 billion in 1998.[20]

Box–Office Revenues

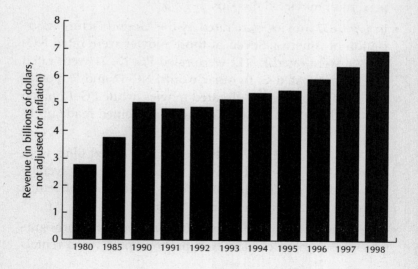

Box–Office Revenues

Year	Revenue (in billions of dollars, not adjusted for inflation)
1980	2.75
1985	3.75
1990	5.02
1991	4.80
1992	4.87
1993	5.15
1994	5.39
1995	5.49
1996	5.91
1997	6.37
1998	6.95

- Although Americans aged 12 to 24 make up about 20 percent of the total U.S. population, they accounted for 37.4 percent of movie admissions in 1998.[21]

- In 1998, 657 movies were rated by the Motion Picture Association of America. Seven of those movies were rated NC–17; 428 were rated R; 112 were rated PG–13; 71 were rated PG; 39 were rated G. In other words, NC–17 and R movies made up 66 percent of all rated movies, while PG–13 made up 17 percent and PG and G movies combined made up 17 percent.[22]

- Between 1988 and 1997, 17.4 times more R–rated films were produced than G–rated films. At the same time, the average G–rated film produced a 78 percent greater rate of return than the average R–rated film.[23]

- Americans spend more than $9 billion a year on pornography. The number of hard–core pornographic video rentals increased from 75 million in 1985, to 490 million in 1992, to 686 million in 1998.[24]

- The U.S. "adult" cable and satellite industries generate $310 million in annual revenue.[25]

RECREATION AND LEISURE

- **Between 1990 and 1998, music unit sales* increased 29 percent. But between 1973 and 1998, sales have increased more than 80 percent.**

Music Units Sold

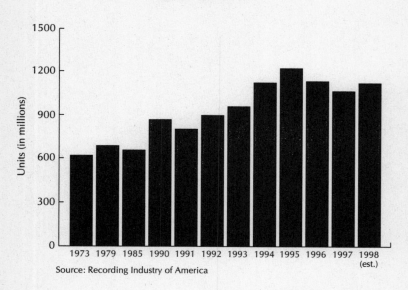

Source: Recording Industry of America

* Music units include CDs, CD singles, cassettes, cassette singles, LPs/EPs, vinyl singles, and music videos.

Music Units Sold

Year	Units (in millions)
1973	616
1979	683
1985	653
1990	866
1991	801
1992	896
1993	956
1994	1,123
1995	1,223
1996	1,113
1997	1,063
1998	1,120 (est.)

Source: Recording Industry of America.

Factual Overview: Music and Radio

- In 1997, Americans spent $12 billion on music.[26]

- Eighty-seven percent of 13-to-17-year-olds listen to music after school.[27]

- At least 95 percent of all teenagers and adults listen to the radio every week.[28]

- In 1998, rock music (25.7 percent) and country music (14.1 percent) consumers continued to purchase the most amount of music; R&B consumers took up 12.8 percent of the market; pop music 10 percent, rap music 9.7 percent, gospel 6.3 percent, classical music 3.3 percent, and jazz music 1.9 percent.[29]

- Between 1985 and 1997, the Rolling Stones accounted for three of the top four highest-grossing North American concert tours.[30]

Top–Grossing North American Concert Tours, 1985–97

Artist	Year	Gross (in millions of dollars, not adjusted for inflation)	Cities/ Shows
Rolling Stones	1994	121.2	43/60
Pink Floyd	1994	103.5	39/59
Rolling Stones	1989	98.0	33/60
Rolling Stones	1997	89.3	26/33
U2	1997	79.9	37/46
The Eagles	1994	79.4	32/54
New Kids on the Block	1990	74.1	122/152
U2	1992	67.0	61/73
The Eagles	1995	63.3	46/58
Barbra Streisand	1994	58.9	6/22

Factual Overview: Books, Computers, and the Internet

- The average American buys more than twice as many books today as in 1947.[31] At the same time, Americans devote almost five times as much time to watching television and videotapes as they do to reading.[32]

- From 1990 to 1997, overall newspaper circulation dropped from 62.5 million to 58.4 million.[33] The percentage of American families who subscribe to a daily newspaper dropped from 50 percent in 1997 to 44 percent in 1998.[34]

- In 1993, 3 million people were connected to the Internet, compared to roughly 80 million in 1999.[35]

- About half of all teenagers use computers to go on–line, mostly to use e–mail.[36]

- Between 1995 and 1998, the number of U.S. homes using the Internet increased 237 percent.[37]

U.S. Homes Using the Internet

Year	Number of Homes (in millions)
1995	9.4
1996	15.2
1997	21.8
1998	31.7

- Sixty-nine percent of families with children own or rent electronic video games. The average child plays those video games seven hours a week.[38]

Factual Overview: Leisure and Spending

- In 1998, the average American spent 99.5 percent of his after-tax income. This dropped Americans' personal-savings rate, which is personal savings as a percentage of disposable income, to its lowest level since World War II.[39]

Americans' Personal-Savings Rate

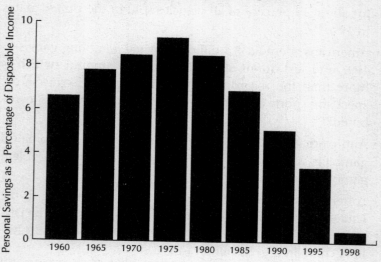

Americans' Personal–Savings Rate

Year	Savings Rate
1960	6.6
1965	7.8
1970	8.5
1975	9.3
1980	8.5
1985	6.9
1990	5.1
1995	3.4
1998	0.5

- Thirty–one percent of families in which both parents work are making more than $70,000 a year in income.[40]

- In 1998, teenagers spent around $141 billion, or $4,548 each, on various goods and services.[41]

- Luxury automobiles that cost more than $30,000 accounted for about 12 percent of all vehicles sold in the United States in 1996.[42]

- Americans spent $638.6 billion on legal gambling games in 1997 and lost about $51 billion of that amount (which is more than the recording, video–game, movie, cruise–ship, spectator–sport, and theme–park business revenues combined).[43]

- Approximately 2.5 million adult Americans are pathological gamblers; another 3 million have been classified as problem gamblers.[44]

- Lotteries are the most widespread form of gambling in the United States and operate in thirty–seven states and the District of Columbia. Total lottery sales in 1996 were $42.9 billion, compared to $4 billion in 1982.[45]

CHURCH MEMBERSHIP

- *Between 1990 and 1997, church membership as a percentage of the population has increased slightly. Between 1960 and 1997, the percentage decreased slightly.*

Church Membership

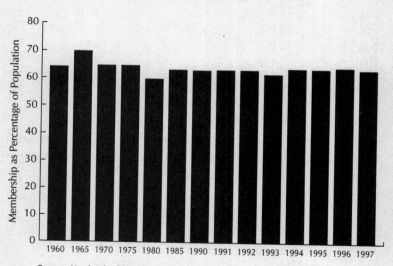

Source: *Yearbook of American and Canadian Churches*

Church Membership

Year	Members (in millions)	Membership as Percentage of Population
1960	114.4	63.8
1965	124.7	69.5
1970	131.0	64.4
1975	131.0	64.4
1980	134.8	59.5
1985	142.9	63.0
1990	156.3	62.8
1991	156.6	63.0
1992	156.6	63.0
1993	153.1	61.5
1994	158.2	63.6
1995	158.0	63.5
1996	159.5	64.1
1997	157.5	63.3

Source: *Yearbook of American and Canadian Churches*

Factual Overview: Religion

• About half of Americans who say they are religious and consider spirituality important in their life attend religious services less than once a month or never.[46]

Religious Affiliations I[47]

Religion	Percent of U.S. Population
Protestant	58
Catholic	26
Jewish	2
Other	6
None	8

Religious Affiliations II[48]

Religion	Number (in millions)
Christian	241.1
Jewish	3.9
Muslim	3.3
New-Religionists	1.4
Hindus	1.3

- In 1997, Gallup replicated a survey it originally conducted in 1947. It found that the same percentage of Americans pray (90 percent), believe in God (96 percent), and attend church once a week.[49]

**Americans Who Say Religion Is
Very Important in Their Life[50]**

Year	Very important (percent who say)	Not very important (percent who say)
1965	70	7
1978	52	14
1985	55	13
1990	58	13
1998	62	12

- In 1994, 18 percent of Americans said they considered themselves members of the religious right. A higher proportion of blacks than whites thought of themselves as members of the religious right (30 percent versus 17 percent).[51]

- Black Americans are more likely to consider themselves "born again" (51 percent of blacks and 36 percent of the general population), to be a church member (82 percent and 69 percent), to attend church weekly (43 percent and 32 percent), and to view religion as a solution to today's problems (86 percent and 62 percent).[52]

- The South leads all regions of the country in the proportion of people who say they take their religion very seriously (69 percent). The West ranks last among regions (48 percent).[53]

- Until the late 1980s, organized religion enjoyed the highest confidence of the American public, leading all other institutions in which they had a great deal of confidence. Two out of three Americans named the church as an institution in which they placed the utmost trust. Today, slightly more than half of all Americans say they place great trust in organized religion, which makes the military and the police the institutions most trusted by Americans.[54]

- Teen churchgoing has remained relatively constant since 1980. About half of all teenagers attend a religious service in an average week.[55]

- Ninety-six percent of Americans profess a belief in God or a "universal spirit"; 90 percent believe in heaven, and 77 percent rate their chance of going to heaven as excellent or good; 73 percent believe in hell; 65 percent in the devil.[56]

DEPRESSION

- *More people die from suicide than from homicide in the United States. Between 1990 and 1996, 216,631 Americans committed suicide. During the same time, there were 161,020 murders committed in the United States.*

Suicides

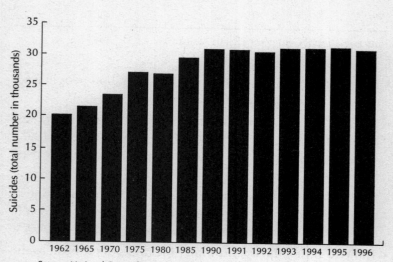

Source: National Center for Health Statistics

Suicides

Year	Total Number	Suicide Rate (per 100,000)
1962	20,203	11.0
1965	21,501	11.4
1970	23,480	11.8
1975	27,063	12.5
1980	26,869	11.3
1985	29,453	11.5
1990	30,906	11.5
1991	30,810	11.3
1992	30,484	11.1
1993	31,102	11.2
1994	31,142	11.2
1995	31,284	11.1
1996	30,903	10.8

Source: National Center for Health Statistics

- In the United States in 1998, roughly 18 million people were afflicted with depression.[57]

- Sales of the antidepressant medication Prozac totaled $2.8 billion in 1998, an increase of 10 percent from 1997.[58] Between 1987 and 1997, about 18 million Americans used Prozac.[59]

- In 1996, 8,000 children under 6 years old were using one of three commonly prescribed antidepressants—Prozac, Zoloft, or Paxil. That number rose 400 percent, to 40,000, in 1997.[60]

- The World Health Organization now ranks depression as the developed world's most disabling disease for women.[61]

- Over the past thirty years, psychology journals have published 45,000 articles about depression and 400 on happiness.[62]

NOTES

[1] Nielsen Media Research, "1998 Report on Television."

[2] Ibid.

[3] Ibid.

[4] Annenberg Public Policy Center, University of Pennsylvania, "Media in the Home 1999: The Fourth Annual Survey of Parents and Children."

[5] Nielsen Media Research, "1998 Report on Television."

[6] Ibid.

[7] Annenberg Public Policy Center, University of Pennsylvania, "Media in the Home 1999: The Fourth Annual Survey of Parents and Children."

[8] Ibid.

[9] Urie Bronfenbrenner, Peter McClelland, Elaine Wethington, Phyllis Moen, and Stephen J. Ceci, *The State of Americans* (New York: The Free Press, 1996).

[10] Annenberg Policy Center, University of Pennsylvania, "Media in the Home 1999: The Fourth Annual Survey of Parents and Children."

[11] Pew Research Center for the People and the Press, April/May 1998, cited in William Powers, "That's Not Entertainment," *National Journal*, January 16, 1999, and Karyln Bowman, "Media Consumption Habits," *American Enterprise*, March/April 1999.

[12] Television survey by the Center for Media and Public Affairs, September 1996.

[13] Ibid.

[14] Robert Lichter, Linda Lichter, Stanley Rothman, and Daniel Amundson, cited in Jim Impoco, *U.S. News & World Report*, April 15, 1996.

[15] "Sex on TV: Content and Context," Biennial Report to the Kaiser Family Foundation, February 1999.

[16] "Unintended Consequences: With Ratings System in Place, TV More Offensive Than Ever," Parents Television Council, May 1999.

[17] Wade F. Horn and National Fatherhood Institute, cited in Cheryl Wetzstein, *Washington Times*, March 3, 1999.

[18] *Business Week*, 1997, cited in "Fact Sheet," National Institute on Media and the Family.

[19] Television survey by the Center for Media and Public Affairs, August 1997.

[20] Motion Picture Association of America, "1998 U.S. Economic Review."

[21] Ibid.

[22] Ibid.

[23] "Profitability Study of MPAA Rated Movies Released during 1988–1997," Seidman School of Business, December 1, 1998, commissioned by the Dove Foundation.

[24] Richard C. Morais, "Porn Goes Public," *Forbes*, June 14, 1999; Eric Schlosser, "The Business of Pornography," *U.S. News & World Report*, April 10, 1997; James Laslow, "Internet Helps Boost Adult Video Sales to Record High," *Adult Video News*, May 26, 1999.

[25] Ibid.

[26] P. G. Christenson and D. F. Roberts, *It's Not Only Rock & Roll: Popular Music in the Lives of Adolescents* (New Jersey: Hampton Press, 1998), cited in "Substance Use in Popular Movies and Music," April 1999, Office of National Drug Control Policy and the U.S. Department of Health and Human Services.

[27] Ibid.

[28] Arbitron National Database, "Radio Today: How America Listens to Radio," 1998 edition.

[29] Recording Industry of America, "1998 Consumer Profile."

[30] *World Almanac* (New Jersey: World Almanac Books, 1999).

[31] Tyler Cowen, "Is Our Culture in Decline?" *CATO Policy Report*, September/October 1998.

[32] Annenberg Public Policy Center, University of Pennsylvania, "Television in the Home 1998: The Third Annual National Survey of Parents and Children."

[33] Newspaper Association of America, "Veronis, Suhler & Associates Communications Industry Forecast."

[34] Annenberg Public Policy Center, University of Pennsylvania, "Television in the Home 1998: The Third Annual National Survey of Parents and Children."

[35] U.S. Department of Commerce, cited in University of Texas Center for Research in Electronic Commerce, "The Internet Economy Indicators," June 1999.

[36] Barbara Kantrowitz and Pat Wingert, "How Well Do You Know Your Kid?" *Newsweek*, May 10, 1999.

[37] Motion Picture Association of America, "1998 U.S. Economic Review."

[38] David Walsh, National Institute on Media and the Family, "1998 Video and Computer Game Report Card," December 1, 1998.

[39] Department of Commerce statistics, cited in Robert J. Samuelson, "Hell No, We Won't Save!" *Washington Post*, February 17, 1999.

[40] Bureau of Labor Statistics, cited in Shannon Brownlee and Matthew Miller, "Lies Parents Tell Themselves About Why They Work," *U.S. News & World Report*, May 12, 1997.

[41] Richard Cohen, "When the Market Gets What It Wants," *Washington Post*, May 21, 1999.

[42] Robert H. Frank, "Our Climb to Sublime," *Washington Post*, January 24, 1999.

[43] Timothy L. O'Brien, "Gambling: Married to the Action, for Better or Worse," *New York Times*, November 8, 1998, and *Business Week*, June 21, 1999.

[44] Report to the National Gambling Impact Study Commission, "Gambling Impact and Behavior Study," April 1, 1999. According to the American Psychiatric Association, "pathological gambling is persistent and recurrent maladaptive gambling behavior...that disrupts personal, family, or vocational pursuits." While pathological gamblers exhibit five or more signs of persistent and recurrent maladaptive gambling behavior, problem gamblers exhibit three or four (National Gambling Impact Study Commission).

[45] National Gambling Impact Study, "Lotteries," *www.ngisc.gov/research/lotteries .html.*

[46] MIDUS survey, cited in Marilyn Elias, "So Much Solemn Faith, So Little Religious Loyalty," *USA Today*, February 16, 1999.

[47] U.S. Department of Commerce, Bureau of the Census, *Statistical Abstract* (Washington, D.C.: GPO, 1998).

[48] *Yearbook of American and Canadian Churches*, edited by Eileen W. Lindner (New York: National Council of the Churches of Christ, 1999).

[49] David Whitman, "More Moral," *New Republic*, February 22, 1999.

[50] CNN/*USA Today*/Gallup poll, June 22–23, 1998.

[51] George H. Gallup, Jr., Princeton Religion Research Center, "Religion in America," 1996 report.

[52] Ibid.

[53] Ibid.

[54] Ibid.

[55] Gallup Religion Data, "Teen Churchgoing Fairly Stable over the Last Two Decades," 1997.

[56] George H. Gallup, Jr., Princeton Religion Research Center, "Religion in America," 1996 report.

[57] Joannie M. Schrof and Stacey Schultz, "Melancholy Nation," *U.S. News & World Report*, March 8, 1999.

[58] Eli Lilly and Company, Lilly Corporate Center, "1998 Annual Report," http://www.lilly.com.

[59] *Focus*, Eli Lilly, Vol. 5, No. 2 (1997).

[60] IMS Health research, cited in "Depressing Numbers," *Washington Times*, May 30, 1999.

[61] World Health Organization, "The Global Burden of Disease," edited by Christopher J. L. Murray and Alan D. Lopez, 1996. The World Health Organization measures "disabling" by the combined burden of various fatal and nonfatal health indicators.

[62] Martin Seligman, cited in Trish Hall, "Seeking a Focus on Joy in Field of Psychology," *New York Times*, April 28, 1998.

CHAPTER SIX

Civic Participation

VOTER TURNOUT

- *In the course of twenty-eight years, between 1960 and 1988, turnout of registered voters dipped below 50 percent six times. But between 1990 and 1998, in the course of eight years, it fell below 50 percent four times.*

Voter Turnout: Presidential Years

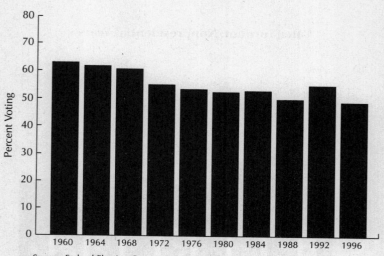

Source: Federal Election Commission

Voter Turnout: Presidential Years

Year	Voting Population (in millions)	Turnout (in millions)	Percent Voting
1960	109.2	68.8	63.1
1964	114.1	70.6	61.9
1968	120.3	73.2	60.8
1972	140.8	77.7	55.2
1976	152.3	81.6	53.6
1980	164.6	86.5	52.6
1984	174.5	92.7	53.1
1988	182.8	91.6	50.1
1992	189.5	104.4	55.1
1996	196.5	96.5	49.1

Source: Federal Election Commission

Voter Turnout: Nonpresidential Years

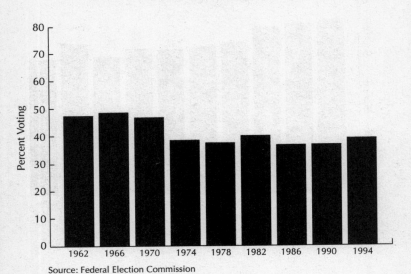

Source: Federal Election Commission

Voter Turnout: Nonpresidential Years

Year	Voting Population (in millions)	Turnout (in millions)	Percent Voting
1962	112.4	53.1	47.3
1966	116.1	56.2	48.4
1970	124.5	58.0	46.6
1974	146.3	55.9	38.2
1978	158.4	58.9	37.2
1982	169.9	67.6	39.8
1986	178.6	64.9	36.4
1990	185.8	67.9	36.5
1994	193.7	75.1	38.8

Source: Federal Election Commission

Factual Overview: Voter Turnout

- More Americans are registered to vote than ever before. In 1998, there was an increase of 5.5 million registered voters since 1996. Nevertheless, the rate of voter turnout hit its lowest point in more than fifty years when it dropped to 36.1 percent of eligible voters in 1998.[1]

- In every election since 1972 (a year after the voting age was lowered to 18), less than 45 percent of registered voters aged 18 to 24 have voted.[2]

The States: Voter Turnout

- In 1996, voter turnout was lowest in Nevada and highest in Maine.[3]

States with Lowest Voter Turnout, 1996

State	Percent Voting
Nevada	38.3
Hawaii	40.5
Texas	41.3
South Carolina	41.6
Georgia	42.4

States with Highest Voter Turnout, 1996

State	Percent Voting
Maine	71.9
Minnesota	64.1
Montana	62.1
South Dakota	60.5
Wyoming	59.4

TRUST AND CYNICISM

- **In 1964, 76 percent of Americans thought the government could be trusted always or most of the time. By 1996, the percentage had dropped to 27 percent.**

How much of the time do you think you can trust the government in Washington to do what is right? Just about always, most of the time, or only some of the time?

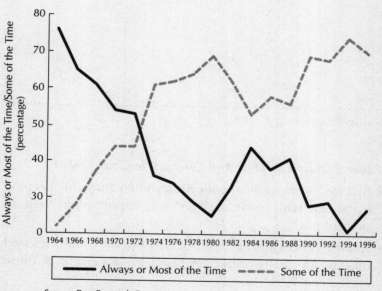

Source: Pew Research Center

How much of the time do you think you can trust the government in Washington to do what is right? Just about always, most of the time, or only some of the time?

Year	Always or Most of the Time (percent)	Some of the time (percent)
1964	76	22
1966	65	28
1968	61	37
1970	54	44
1972	53	44
1974	36	61
1976	34	62
1978	29	64
1980	25	69
1982	33	62
1984	44	53
1986	38	58
1988	41	56
1990	28	69
1992	29	68
1994	21	74
1996	27	70

Source: Pew Research Center

Factual Overview: Trust and Cynicism in Government

- In 1966, 58 percent of college freshmen thought "keeping up to date with political affairs" was important. In 1998, 26 percent did.[4]

- Among Americans aged 18 to 29, 39 percent think elected officials are trustworthy, compared to 56 percent of those aged 65 or older.[5]

- In 1975, nearly 35 percent of U.S. high school seniors agreed with the statement that "most people can be trusted." By 1997, 18 percent agreed.[6]

- The Supreme Court is the only branch of the federal government in which more Americans hold "a great deal" of confidence rather than "hardly any."[7]

- According to a December 1998 poll, Bill Clinton is the man most admired by Americans, outdistancing Pope John Paul II.[8]

Men Most Admired by Americans, 1998

Man	Percent Voting For
President Clinton	18
Pope John Paul II	7
Rev. Billy Graham	5
Michael Jordan	4
President Bush	3
Sen. John Glenn	3
Gen. Colin Powell	3
President Reagan	3

CHARITABLE GIVING

- *Between 1990 and 1998, charitable giving has increased 38 percent in inflation-adjusted dollars. Between 1968 and 1998, charitable giving increased 98 percent in inflation-adjusted dollars.*

Charitable Giving

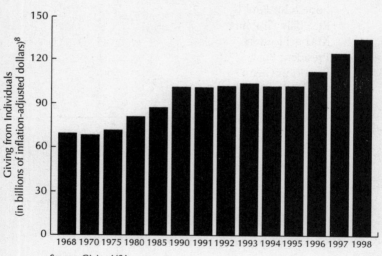

Source: Giving USA

Charitable Giving

Year	Total (in billions of inflation-adjusted dollars)	Giving from Individuals (in billions of inflation-adjusted dollars)
1968	88.3	69.1
1970	88.4	68.0
1975	86.5	71.3
1980	96.2	80.5
1985	108.6	86.9
1990	126.4	101.1
1991	125.7	100.9
1992	128.3	101.9
1993	131.5	103.8
1994	131.1	101.8
1995	132.6	102.0
1996	144.0	111.8
1997	160.2	124.9
1998	174.5	134.8

Source: Giving USA

- Charitable giving rose 9 percent in inflation-adjusted terms from 1997 to 1998, totaling more than $174.5 billion.[9]

- In 1998, 77 percent ($135 billion) of charitable giving came from individuals, 10 percent ($17 billion) from foundations, 8 percent ($14 billion) from bequests, and 5 percent ($9 billion) from corporations.[10]

- In 1998, religious congregations and denominations remained the largest recipient of charitable giving, receiving more than $76 billion in donations, up about 3 percent in inflation-adjusted terms from 1997. Since 1990, charitable giving to religious organizations has increased by 27 percent.[11]

- Nearly 75 percent of U.S. households report some kind of charitable contribution.[12] Eighty-two percent of Americans belong to at least one voluntary association.[13]

- Churchgoers are more involved in charitable activity than nonchurchgoers. They are more likely to do unpaid volunteer work, give money to charity, and donate clothing and other goods to a charitable organization.[14]

- Private- and home-schooling families are more likely than public-schooling families to engage in various forms of civic participation. Nearly 15 percent more have voted in recent elections; 26 percent more private-schooling families than public-schooling families are members of community and volunteer groups.[15]

The States: Charitable Giving*

- In general, residents of southern states devote larger percentages of their income to charity than residents of northern states.[16]

- New England (Connecticut, Maine, Massachusetts, New Hampshire, Rhode Island, and Vermont) earns 6 percent of U.S. income but accounts for 5 percent of total U.S. charitable giving. Conversely, the South Atlantic region (Delaware, Washington, D.C., Florida, Georgia, Maryland, North Carolina, South Carolina, Virginia, and West Virginia) earns 18 percent of the nation's income but accounts for 20 percent of all U.S. charitable giving.[17]

- Of the five states whose residents contribute the least, on average, to charity, four are from New England—Rhode Island, New Hampshire, Vermont, and Maine.[18]

---

* To read more about how comparisons are made among states and levels of charitable giving, see the "Note to the Reader" in the back of the book.

Charitable Giving, 1996

State	Average Contribution (in dollars)	Total Contributions (in thousands of dollars)
Wyoming	5,822	178,815
Utah	4,845	1,322,259
Tennessee	4,123	1,576,562
District of Columbia	3,952	325,689
Texas	3,702	4,778,669
Arkansas	3,601	661,119
Mississippi	3,531	615,428
Alabama	3,423	1,397,902
Louisiana	3,312	868,929
Florida	3,234	4,536,380
South Dakota	3,191	124,574
Oklahoma	3,069	962,450
Idaho	3,023	387,248
South Carolina	3,012	1,206,735
Georgia	2,998	2,730,975
North Carolina	2,943	2,558,909
New York	2,927	8,007,800
Kansas	2,874	778,245
Nevada	2,784	561,317
North Dakota	2,768	115,728
Nebraska	2,751	476,490
Indiana	2,713	1,558,826
West Virginia	2,682	230,792
Missouri	2,660	1,418,818
Virginia	2,651	2,550,208
Delaware	2,646	291,372
Illinois	2,637	3,888,703
California	2,625	10,888,331
Alaska	2,611	157,012

(continued next page)

State	Average Contribution (in dollars)	Total Contributions (in thousands of dollars)
Washington	2,523	1,683,631
Michigan	2,483	3,055,652
Kentucky	2,439	909,521
Maryland	2,438	2,245,707
Pennsylvania	2,437	3,410,262
Iowa	2,403	717,403
Connecticut	2,398	1,346,498
New Mexico	2,367	329,120
Colorado	2,357	1,323,776
Oregon	2,321	1,013,100
Arizona	2,287	1,219,753
Minnesota	2,283	1,689,868
Ohio	2,227	2,915,438
New Jersey	2,220	3,097,448
Massachusetts	2,118	2,017,949
Wisconsin	2,056	1,458,167
Montana	2,008	182,292
Hawaii	1,904	304,023
Maine	1,821	245,280
Vermont	1,798	121,938
New Hampshire	1,776	282,829
Rhode Island	1,718	241,733

Source: Giving USA

IMMIGRATION

- *The percentage of Americans who are foreign-born nearly doubled between 1960 and 1997.*

Foreign–Born Population

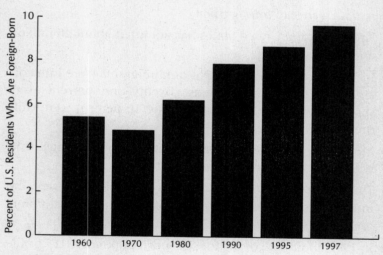

Source: Census Bureau

Foreign–Born Population

Year	Percent of U.S. Residents Who Are Foreign–Born
1960	5.4
1970	4.8
1980	6.2
1990	7.9
1995	8.7
1997	9.7

Source: Census Bureau

Factual Overview: Immigration

- Since 1965, the United States has admitted about 20 million immigrants.[19]

- In 1997, more than 40 percent of immigrants were immediate relatives of U.S. citizens. Twenty-one percent were spouses. 9 percent were parents, and 10 percent were children of U.S. citizens.[20]

- More than 70 percent of immigrants are over the age of 18 when they arrive in the United States.[21]

- Three states—California, New York, and Florida—were the intended residence of more than 50 percent of legal immigrants in 1997.[22]

- In 1997, about half of the foreign-born population (13.1 million) were natives of Central America, South America, and the Caribbean. Of these, more than half (7 million) listed Mexico as their birthplace.[23]

- Within ten years of arriving in the United States, more than three out of four immigrants spoke English well or very well in 1990. Less than 2 percent of forty-year-plus immigrants spoke no English at all.[24]

- During the 1990s, immigration was responsible for almost half of all population growth in the United States.[25]

Immigration as a Percentage of Total Population Growth

Period	As Percentage of Population Growth
1960–64	12.5
1965–69	19.7
1970–80	19.4
1981–90	32.8
1991–96	47.1

- The rate of immigration has increased since the 1960s.[26]

Immigration Rate

Period	Total Immigrants	Rate (per 1,000 U.S. population)
1961–70	3,321,677	1.7
1971–80	4,493,314	2.1
1981–90	7,338,062	2.9
1991–96	6,146,213	2.3

- More than 20 percent of the recipients of the Congressional Medal of Honor in American wars have been immigrants.[27]

Factual Overview: Illegal Immigration

- There were around 5 million illegal immigrants residing in the United States in 1996, which means they made up nearly 2 percent of the total population.[28]

- Mexico is the source of more than half (54 percent) of all illegal immigrants. The undocumented Mexican population has grown at an average of more than 150,000 a year since 1988.[29]

- More than 2 million (40 percent) of all illegal immigrants residing in the United States entered the country legally on a temporary basis but then failed to depart.[30]

MILITARY SERVICE

- *Between 1990 and 1998, the number of Americans on active duty in the Navy, Marines, Army, and Air Force has declined 32 percent—from 2.1 million to 1.4 million. Between 1960 and 1998, the number dropped 44 percent—from 2.5 million to 1.4 million.*

Americans Active in Military

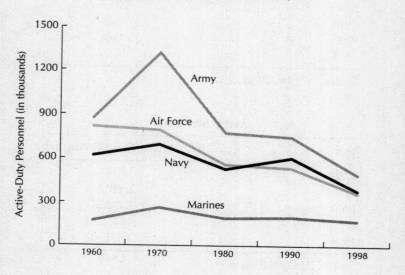

Navy Strength

Year	Active–Duty Personnel
1960	617,984
1970	692,660
1980	527,200
1990	604,562
1998	381,203

Source: *The World Almanac*

Marines Strength

Year	Active–Duty Personnel
1960	170,621
1970	259,737
1980	188,469
1990	196,652
1998	172,632

Source: *The World Almanac*

Army Strength

Year	Active–Duty Personnel
1960	871,348
1970	1,319,735
1980	772,661
1990	746,220
1998	491,707

Source: *The World Almanac*

Air Force Strength

Year	Active–Duty Personnel
1960	814,213
1970	791,078
1980	557,969
1990	535,233
1998	363,479

Source: *The World Almanac*

Factual Overview: Military Service

• Veterans now make up less than one–tenth of the American population.[31]

Living Veterans

Year	Veterans (in millions)	As Percentage of Population
1960	22.5	12.5
1965	21.8	11.2
1970	27.0	13.2
1975	28.3	13.1
1980	28.6	12.6
1985	28.1	11.8
1990	27.3	10.9
1995	26.2	10.0
1998	25.2	9.2

• Between 1971 and 1999, the number of women on active military duty increased from 42,323 to 191,952. In 1971, women made up 1.6 percent of military personnel. In 1999, they made up more than 14 percent, which is a 780 percent increase since 1971.[32]

NOTES

[1] Curtis Gans, cited in "'98 Voter Turnout Rate Was Lowest in 56 Years," *Washington Post*, February 10, 1999.

[2] Urie Bronfenbrenner, Peter McClelland, Elaine Wethington, Phyllis Moen, and Stephen J. Ceci, *The State of Americans* (New York: The Free Press, 1996).

[3] Federal Election Commission, "Voter Registration and Turnout," 1996.

[4] L. J. Sax, A. W. Astin, W. S. Korn, and K. M. Mahoney, "The American Freshman: National Norms for Fall 1998," Los Angeles: Higher Education Research Institute, UCLA.

[5] William A. Galston, "Where We Stand," *Blueprint: Ideas for a New Century*, Spring 1999.

[6] Urie Bronfenbrenner, Peter McClelland, Elaine Wethington, Phyllis Moen, and Stephen J. Ceci, *The State of Americans* (New York: The Free Press, 1996).

[7] Francis Fukuyama, *The Great Disruption* (New York: The Free Press, 1999).

[8] Lydia Saad, the Gallup Organization, December 1998.

[9] AAFRC Trust for Philanthropy, "Giving USA: 1999," Annual Report on Philanthropy for the Year 1998.

[10] Ibid.

[11] Ibid.

[12] Century Foundation report, cited in Geneva Overholser, "Let the Giving Grow," *Washington Post*, February 10, 1999.

[13] William A. Galston, "Where We Stand," *Blueprint: Ideas for a New Century*, Spring 1999.

[14] George H. Gallup, Jr., Princeton Religion Research Center, "Religion in America," 1996 report.

[15] U.S. Department of Education, National Center for Education Statistics 1996 National Household Survey, cited in "Is Private School Privatizing," *First Things*, April 1999.

[16] AAFRC Trust for Philanthropy, "Giving USA Update," Issue 3, 1998.

[17] Ibid.

[18] Ibid.

[19] John J. Miller, *The Unmaking of Americans* (New York: The Free Press, 1998).

[20] U.S. Department of Justice, Immigration and Naturalization Service, "Annual Report: Legal Immigration, Fiscal Year 1997."

[21] National Immigration Forum, "Facts on Immigration and the Economy," January 1999.

[22] U.S. Department of Justice, Immigration and Naturalization Service, "Annual Report: Legal Immigration, Fiscal Year 1997."

[23] *The New York Times Almanac* (New York: Penguin Putnam, 1999).

[24] National Immigration Forum, Executive Summary "From Newcomers to New Americans," 1999.

[25] *The New York Times Almanac* (New York: Penguin Putnam, 1999).

[26] Ibid.

[27] Stuart Anderson, "In Defense of a Nation: The Military Contributions of Immigrants," American Immigration Law Foundation and Empower America, 1996.

[28] U.S. Department of Justice, Immigration and Naturalization Service, "Illegal Alien Resident Population," *www.ins.usdog.gov/stats/illegalalien/index.html.*

[29] Ibid.

[30] Ibid.

[31] Department of Veterans Affairs, VA Office of Information Management and Statistics, unpublished information.

[32] Department of Defense, Manpower Data Center, June 10, 1999, unpublished information.

CHAPTER SEVEN

International Comparisons

VIOLENT CRIME

- *Violent crime rates in the United States remain among the highest in the industrialized world, although they are substantially lower than rates in New Zealand and Canada.*

Violent Crime Rates

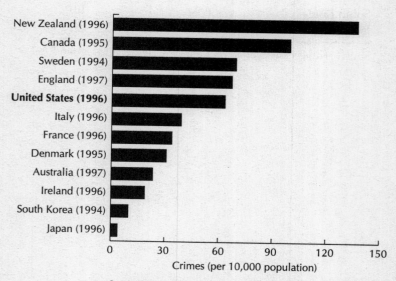

Source: Francis Fukuyama, *The Great Disruption*, Figures 2.1 and A-1

Violent Crime Rates

Country	Year	Rate (per 10,000)
New Zealand	1996	137.1
Canada	1995	99.5
Sweden	1994	69.4
England	1997	67.2
United States	**1996**	**63.4**
Italy	1996	39.1
France	1996	34.0
Denmark	1995	30.9
Australia	1997	23.4
Ireland	1996	19.0
South Korea	1994	10.0
Japan	1996	4.1

Source: Francis Fukuyama, *The Great Disruption*, Figures 2.1 and A-1

MARRIAGE

- **The United States has the highest marriage rate in the industrialized world.**

Marriage Rates, 1995

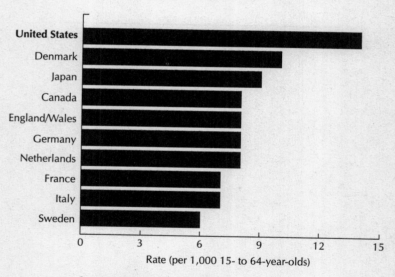

Rate (per 1,000 15- to 64-year-olds)

Source: *Statistical Abstract*, Table 1346

Marriage Rates, 1995

Country	Rate (per 1,000 15- to 64-year-olds)
United States	**14**
Denmark	10
Japan	9
Canada	8
England/Wales	8
Germany	8
Netherlands	8
France	7
Italy	7
Sweden	6

Source: *Statistical Abstract,* Table 1346

DIVORCE

- *The United States has the highest divorce rate in the industrialized world.*

Divorce Rates, 1995

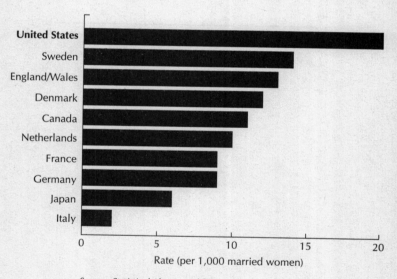

Rate (per 1,000 married women)

Source: *Statistical Abstract,* Table 1346

Divorce Rates, 1995

Country	Rate (per 1,000 married women)
United States	**20**
Sweden	14
England/Wales	13
Denmark	12
Canada	11
Netherlands	10
France	9
Germany	9
Japan	6
Italy	2

Source: *Statistical Abstract,* Table 1346

OUT-OF-WEDLOCK BIRTHS

- *The U.S. out-of-wedlock birth rate is lower than that of Sweden, Denmark, France, and England/Wales.*

Births to Unmarried Women, 1995

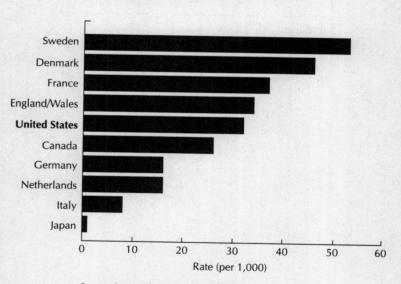

Rate (per 1,000)

Source: *Statistical Abstract*, Table 1347

Births to Unmarried Women, 1995

Country	Rate (per 1,000)
Sweden	53
Denmark	46
France	37
England/Wales	34
United States	**32**
Canada	26
Germany	16
Netherlands	16
Italy	8
Japan	1

Source: *Statistical Abstract*, Table 1347

SINGLE-PARENT FAMILIES

• *The United States has the highest percentage of single-parent families in the industrialized world.*

Single–Parent Families

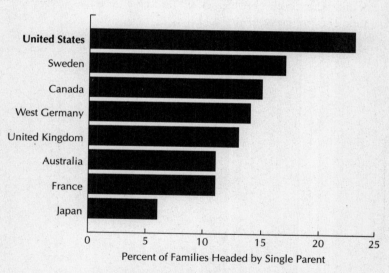

Percent of Families Headed by Single Parent

Source: Urie Bronfenbrenner, et al., *The State of Americans* (New York: The Free Press, 1996)

Single–Parent Families

Country	Percent of Families Headed by Single Parent
United States	**23**
Sweden	17
Canada	15
West Germany	14
United Kingdom	13
Australia	11
France	11
Japan	6

Source: Urie Bronfenbrenner, et al., *The State of Americans* (New York: The Free Press, 1996)

ABORTION

- ***The abortion rate in the United States is the highest in the industrialized world.****

Abortion Rates

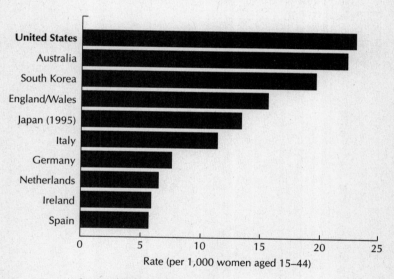

Rate (per 1,000 women aged 15–44)

Source: Alan Guttmacher Institute

* Cuba (77.7), Russia (68.4), China (26.1), and Mexico (25.1) all have higher rates of abortion than the United States, but they are not usually considered developed nations.

Abortion Rates

Country	Rate (per 1,000 women aged 15–44)
United States (1996)	**22.9**
Australia (1996)	22.2
South Korea (1996)	19.6
England/Wales (1996)	15.6
Japan (1995)	13.4
Italy (1996)	11.4
Germany (1996)	7.6
Netherlands (1996)	6.5
Ireland (1996)	5.9
Spain (1996)	5.7

Source: Alan Guttmacher Institute

SEXUALLY TRANSMITTED DISEASES

- *The rates of sexually transmitted diseases are several times higher in the United States than rates in other developed countries.*

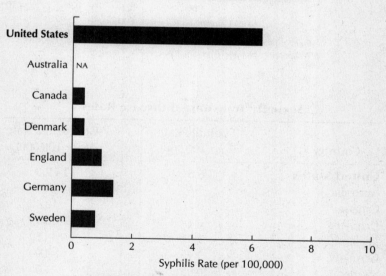

Sexually Transmitted Disease Rates

Syphilis Rate (per 100,000)

Source: Thomas R. Eng and William T. Butler, eds., *The Hidden Epidemic* (Washington: National Academy Press, 1997)

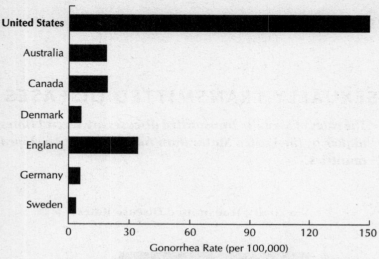

Gonorrhea Rate (per 100,000)

Source: Thomas R. Eng and William T. Butler, eds., *The Hidden Epidemic* (Washington: National Academy Press, 1997)

Sexually Transmitted Disease Rates

Country	Syphillis Rate (per 100,000)	Gonorrhea Rate (per 100,000)
United States	**6.3**	**149.5**
Australia	NA	18.1
Canada	0.4	18.6
Denmark	0.4	5.5
England	1.0	34.1
Germany	1.4	4.9
Sweden	0.8	3.0

Source: Thomas R. Eng and William T. Butler, eds., *The Hidden Epidemic* (Washington: National Academy Press, 1997)

TEENAGE BIRTH RATES

- *The United States has the highest teenage birth rate in the industrialized world. It also has the highest percentage of teenage mothers who are unmarried—76 percent.*

Teenage Birth Rates for Selected Developed Countries

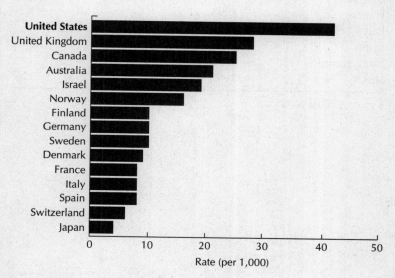

Source: United Nations

Teenage Birth Rates for Selected Developed Countries

Country	Year	Rate (per 1,000 girls, aged 15–19 years old)
United States*	**1997**	**42**
United Kingdom	1995	28
Canada	1994	25
Australia	1995	21
Israel	1994	19
Norway	1992	16
Finland	1995	10
Germany	1995	10
Sweden	1994	10
Denmark	1995	9
France	1993	8
Italy	1991	8
Spain	1994	8
Switzerland	1995	6
Japan	1995	4

Source: United Nations

* The updated U.S. teenage birth rate comes from the U.S. Department of Health and Human Services. Similar updates were not available for other nations.

CHILD POVERTY

- *The child-poverty rate in the United States is among the highest in the developed world.*

Child Poverty

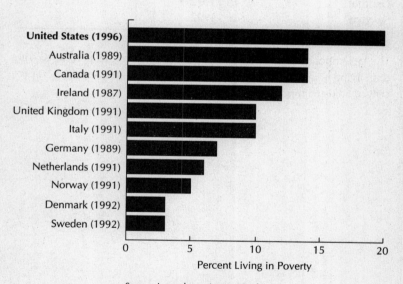

Source: Luxembourg Income Study

Child Poverty

Country	Year	Percent Living In
United States*	**1996**	**20**
Australia	1989	14
Canada	1991	14
Ireland	1987	12
United Kingdom	1991	10
Italy	1991	10
Germany	1989	7
Netherlands	1991	6
Norway	1991	5
Denmark	1992	3
Sweden	1992	3

Source: Luxembourg Income Study

The Luxembourg Income Study defines child poverty as percent of children living in families with adjusted disposable incomes less than 50 percent of adjusted median income for all persons.

* The updated U.S. child–poverty rate comes from the *Statistical Abstract*. Similar updates were not available for other nations.

DRUG USE

- *A larger percentage of American students use illegal drugs than in any other industrialized country.*

Lifetime Illegal Drug Use Among Students Aged 15–16

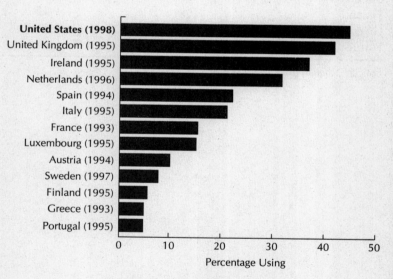

Source: *Monitoring the Future,* 1998

Lifetime Illegal Drug Use Among Students Aged 15–16

Country	Year	Percent Using
United States	**1998**	**44.9**
United Kingdom	1995	42.0
Ireland	1995	37.0
Netherlands	1996	31.7
Spain	1994	22.1
Italy	1995	21.0
France	1993	15.3
Luxembourg	1995	15.0
Austria	1994	9.9
Sweden	1997	7.6
Finland	1995	5.5
Greece	1993	4.8
Portugal	1995	4.7

Source: *Monitoring the Future,* 1998

TELEVISION

- *Twenty-one percent of American 9-year-olds watch more than five hours of televison per weekday—the highest percentage in the developed world.*

Youth Television Watching

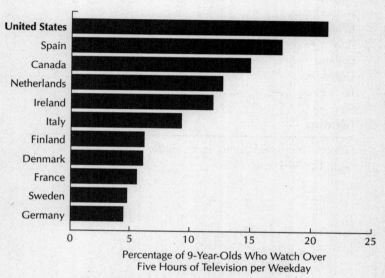

Percentage of 9-Year-Olds Who Watch Over
Five Hours of Television per Weekday

Source: Urie Bronfenbrenner et al., *The State of Americans*
(New York: The Free Press, 1996)

Youth Television Watching

Country	Percent of 9–year–olds Who Watch More Than 5 Hours of Television per Weekday
United States	**21.3**
Spain	17.5
Canada	14.9
Netherlands	12.6
Ireland	11.8
Italy	9.2
Finland	6.1
Denmark	6.0
France	5.5
Sweden	4.7
Germany	4.4

Source: Urie Bronfenbrenner, et al., *The State of Americans* (New York: The Free Press, 1996)

EDUCATION

- *In mathematics and science, American students in the fourth grade are competitive with students from other countries; they are slightly below average in the eighth grade; by the twelfth grade, they are significantly below average.*

Mathematics Scores

The Third International Mathematics and Science Study, 1996

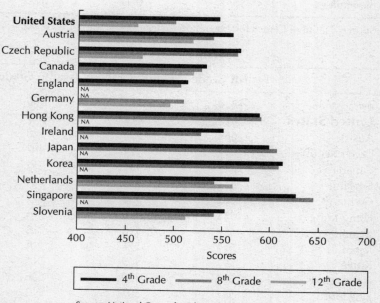

Source: National Center for Education Statistics, "Pursuing Excellence"

Mathematics Scores

	Fourth Grade	Eighth Grade	Twelfth Grade
Average score	529	513	500
United States	**545**	**500**	**461**
Austria	559	539	518
Czech Republic	567	564	466
Canada	532	527	519
England	513	506	NA
Germany	NA	509	495
Hong Kong	587	588	NA
Ireland	550	527	NA
Japan	597	605	NA
Korea	611	607	NA
Netherlands	577	541	560
Singapore	625	643	NA
Slovenia	552	541	512

Source: National Center for Education Statistics, "Pursuing Excellence"

Science Scores

	Fourth Grade	Eighth Grade	Twelfth Grade
Average score	524	516	500
United States	**565**	**534**	**480**
Austria	565	558	520
Czech Republic	557	574	487
Canada	549	531	532
England	551	552	NA
Germany	NA	531	497
Hong Kong	533	522	NA
Ireland	539	538	NA
Japan	574	571	NA
Korea	597	565	NA
Netherlands	557	560	558
Singapore	547	607	NA
Slovenia	546	560	517

Source: National Center for Education Statistics, "Pursuing Excellence"

Annual Expenditure per Student, 1994: Primary

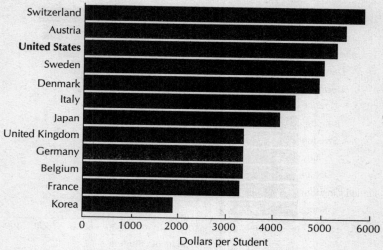

Source: Organization for Economic Cooperation and Development,
"Education at a Glance," Table I

Annual Expenditure per Student, 1994: Primary

Country	Expenditure (in U.S. dollars)
Switzerland	5,860
Austria	5,480
United States	**5,300**
Sweden	5,030
Denmark	4,930
Italy	4,430
Japan	4,110
United Kingdom	3,360
Germany	3,350
Belgium	3,350
France	3,280
Korea	1,890

Source: Organization for Economic Cooperation and Development, "Education at a Glance," Table I

Annual Expenditure per Student, 1994: Secondary

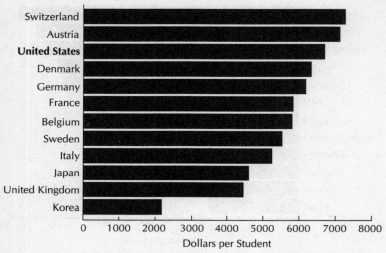

Source: Organization for Economic Cooperation and Development,
"Education at a Glance," Table I

Annual Expenditure per Student, 1994: Secondary

Country	Expenditure (in U.S. dollars)
Switzerland	7,250
Austria	7,100
United States	**6,680**
Denmark	6,310
Germany	6,160
France	5,810
Belgium	5,780
Sweden	5,500
Italy	5,220
Japan	4,580
United Kingdom	4,430
Korea	2,170

Source: Organization for Economic Cooperation and Development, "Education at a Glance," Table I

Factual Overview: An International Education Comparison

Expected Number of Years of
Formal Schooling, 1995

Country	School Life Expectancy
Canada	17.5
New Zealand	16.4
United Kingdom	16.3
Australia	16.2
United States	**15.8**
Belgium	15.5
Finland	15.5
Netherlands	15.5
Spain	15.5

Source: United Nations, "Indicators on Education"

Percentage of the Population Completing
Secondary Education, 1994

Country	Adults Who Completed Secondary School (percent of 25- to 64-year-olds)
United States	**85.1**
Germany	84.0
Switzerland	82.2
Norway	80.7
United Kingdom	74.5
Canada	74.1
Sweden	72.3

Source: National Center for Education Statistics, "The Condition of Education 1997," Table 23-1

Ratio of Students to Teaching Staff, 1996: Primary

Country	Students to Teaching Staff
Korea	31.2
United Kingdom	21.3
Germany	20.9
Japan	19.7
France	19.5
United States	**16.9**
Switzerland	15.9
Austria	12.7
Sweden	12.7
Denmark	11.2
Italy	11.2

Source: Organization for Economic Cooperation and Development, "Education Database," Table B7.1

Ratio of Students to Teaching Staff, 1996: Secondary

Country	Students to Teaching Staff
Korea	24.3
United States	**16.1**
Japan	15.9
United Kingdom	15.6
Germany	15.0
Sweden	13.7
France	13.3
Switzerland	12.3
Denmark	11.0
Italy	10.2
Austria	8.9

Source: Organization for Economic Cooperation and Development, "Education Database," Table B7.1

CHAPTER EIGHT

Decade by Decade

• *Below are tables that compare social trends by decade. Some of the tables provide for aggregate numbers (e.g., the number of crimes and divorces in a decade). Other tables (for example, students per teacher and teenage drug use) trace trends through the decades.*

Crime

Total Crimes

Decade	Number of Total Crimes during the Decade	Rate (crimes per 100,000 residents) in the First Year of Each Decade
1960s	54,009,700	1,906
1970s	106,301,900	4,165
1980s	132,190,700	5,858
1990s (1991–97)	97,977,100	5,898
1997	13,175,070	4,923

Violent Crimes

Decade	Number of Violent Crimes during the Decade	Rate (violent crimes per 100,000 residents) in the First Year of Each Decade
1960s	4,585,290	168
1970s	10,213,630	396
1980s	14,549,940	694
1990s (1991–97)	12,749,830	768
1997	1,634,773	611

(continued next page)

Murders

Decade	Number of Murders during the Decade	Rate (murders per 100,000 residents) in the First Year of Each Decade
1960s	113,070	4.8
1970s	199,270	8.6
1980s	206,840	9.8
1990s (1991–97)	155,790	9.8
1997	18,209	6.8

Family

Out-of-Wedlock Births

Decade	Number of Out–of–Wedlock Births during the Decade	Rate (number of births to unmarried women per 1,000 live births) in the First Year of Each Decade
1960s	3,030,800	56
1970s	4,869,147	113
1980s	8,814,596	189
1990s (1991–97)	8,740,135	295
1997	1,257,444	324

(continued next page)

Divorces

Decade	Number of Divorces during the Decade	Rate (divorces per 1,000 married women) in the First Year of Each Decade
1960s	5,137,000	9.6
1970s	10,220,000	15.8
1980s	11,750,000	22.6
1990s (1991–97)	8,264,000	20.9
1997	1,163,000	19.8

Education

Total Spending on Education—All Levels (Elementary, Secondary, and Higher Education), Public and Private

Decade	Total Spending on Education (in constant dollars)
1960s	NA
1970s	321,775,289,000
1980s	386,256,737,000
1990s (1991–97)	363,096,167,000
1997	559,500,000

Students per Teacher—Public Elementary and Secondary

Year	Number of Students per Teacher
1960	25.8
1965	24.7
1970	22.3
1975	20.4

(continued next page)

Year	Number of Students per Teacher
1980	18.7
1985	17.9
1990	17.2
1995	17.3
1998	17.2

High School Performance—Reading

Year	Average High School Senior Score on NAEP Reading Test
1971	285.2
1975	285.6
1980	285.5
1984	288.8
1988	290.1
1990	290.2
1992	289.7
1994	288.1
1996	286.9

High School Performance—Mathematics

Year	Average High School Senior Score on NAEP Mathematics Test
1973	304
1978	300
1982	299
1986	302
1990	305
1992	307
1994	306
1996	307

Youth Behavior

High School Drug Use

Year	Percent of High School Seniors Who Have Ever Used Any Illicit Drug	Percent of High School Seniors Who Have Ever Used Marijuana
1975	55.2	47.3
1980	65.4	60.3
1985	60.6	54.2
1990	47.9	40.7
1995	48.4	41.7
1998	.54.1	49.1

Suicide

Teenage Suicide

Decade	Number of Teen Suicides during the Decade	Rate (suicides per 100,000 15- to 19-year-olds) in the First Year of Each Decade
1960s (1962–70)	7,195	1.9
1970s	15,871	6.5
1980s	18,563	8.6
1990s (1991–96)	11,285	11.0
1996	1,817	9.7

Overall Suicide

Decade	Number of Suicides during the Decade	Rate (suicides per 100,000 persons) in the First Year of Each Decade
1960s (1962–70)	192,916	11.0
1970s	263,842	11.84
1980s	296,117	11.49
1990s (1991–96)	185,725	11.32
1996	30,903	10.83

Civic Participation

Voter Turnout in Presidential Elections

Year	Turnout (total number)	Turnout (percent of eligible voters who voted)
1960	68,800,000	63.1
1964	70,600,000	61.9
1968	73,200,000	60.9
1972	77,700,000	55.2
1976	81,600,000	53.6
1980	86,500,000	52.6
1984	92,700,000	53.1
1988	91,600,000	50.1
1992	104,400,000	55.1
1996	96,500,000	49.1

Trust in Government

Year	Percent of Americans Who "trust the government in Washington to do what is right ... always or most of the time"
1964	76
1966	65
1970	54
1976	34
1980	25
1986	38
1990	28
1996	27

Military Service

Year	Total Number of Active–Duty Personnel
1960	2,474,166
1970	3,063,210
1980	2,046,299
1990	2,082,667
1998	1,409,021

Population

Year	Population
1960	180,671,158
1970	205,052,174
1980	227,224,681
1990	249,438,712
1998	270,298,524

NOTE TO THE READER

The Index of Leading Cultural Indicators was written for Americans who are interested in the state and direction of their country. Most of the material speaks for itself and requires no expertise in statistical analysis or the social sciences. Nevertheless, there are a few words, terms, and editorial decisions that need additional explanation.

RATES AND RATIOS

The difference between rates and ratios is an important one. The difference can be explained by looking at teenage out–of–wedlock births (see Chapter 4, "Youth Behavior"). A teenage out–of–wedlock birth *ratio* refers to the *proportion* of children born in a given condition (out–of–wedlock births) to a particular group in question (teenagers). The teenage out–of–wedlock birth *rate*, however, refers to the *average number of children born per 1,000 girls* in the group in question (again teenagers, in this case). The two measures are arithmetically independent: a ratio can be going up while the rate is going down.

For example, during the 1990s the teenage out–of–wedlock birth *rate* decreased from 42.5 in 1990 to 42.2 in 1997. During roughly the same period, however, the teenage out-of-wedlock birth *ratio* increased from 68 percent in 1990 to 76 percent in 1996. So while the number of out-of-wedlock births per 1,000 went down, the proportion of all out-of-wedlock births to *teenagers* went up.

WASHINGTON, D.C.

The *Index* compares America's fifty states and the District of Columbia on a wide array of social indicators. The reader will see that the District of Columbia is at or near the top of several categories: out-of-wedlock births, teen out-of-wedlock births, abortion, teen abortion, total and violent crime, educational underachievement, and welfare. Why include Washington, D.C., when it is not a state? The answer is threefold. Inclusion of the District of Columbia follows the standard statistical practices of the Federal Bureau of Investigation, the Bureau of Justice Statistics, the National Center for Health Statistics, the Centers for Disease Control, and the National Center for Education Statistics. All include the District of Columbia in their state-by-state tables—and since the *Index of Leading Cultural Indicators* makes extensive use of these sources, it seems most prudent to remain consistent with the original sources. Note, too, that an important slice of the American population would be overlooked and undercounted if Washington, D.C., were excluded (this would not happen with other cities, since they are always part of a state). Another benefit to including the District of Columbia in the comparisons is that it gives the reader a sense of how our nation's cities, some of which are more populous than several small states, might stack up against states.

It is important to note, however, that Washington, D.C., compares more favorably when matched against other big cities. For example, the District of Columbia ranks first among states but sixth among cities in the percentage of children who are born to unmarried teenage mothers (see Chapter 4).

MEASURING CRIME

There are two different ways of measuring crime. One is the method used for the Uniform Crime Reports (UCR), compiled by the Federal Bureau of Investigation, and the other is the method used for the National Crime Victimization Survey (NCVS), compiled by the Bureau of Justice Statistics. Both are well respected and widely cited.

The UCR program began in 1929; this is a collection of information on seven crimes (homicide, forcible rape, robbery, aggravated assault, burglary, larceny–theft, and arson) based strictly on reports to the police. The NCVS began in 1973; this is based on household surveys, provides a more detailed analysis of crimes, and collects information on the frequency and nature of crimes regardless of whether they are reported to authorities. The numbers of crimes reported in the NCVS are higher than the number of crimes reported in the UCR because those who are victimized by crime do not always report them to the police.

Many of the graphs in the *Index* use UCR data, primarily because they offer time–trend data not available through the NCVS. For a fuller discussion of the differences between UCR and NCVS, the reader should consult the FBI's *Crime in the United States 1997* (pages 411–12).

CHARITABLE GIVING

Although residents of some states appear to be less generous than residents of other states, a few caveats should be noted. First, charitable giving and overall income levels are closely related. That is why most regions account for similar, though not exact, percentages of U.S. income and total U.S. giving. For instance, the South Atlantic region (made up of eight states and the District of Columbia) earns 18 percent of the nation's income and contributes about 20 percent of all U.S. gifts; New England (made up of six states) earns 6 percent of the nation's wealth and accounts for 5 percent of U.S. giving.

Second, contributions that are itemized on tax returns do not account for all charitable contributions. According to the American Association of Fund–Raising Counsel, "though data for 1996 roughly describe only 29 percent of all tax returns filed, *these returns account for more than 80 percent of 1996 individual charitable contributions*" (AAFRC Trust for Philanthropy, *Giving USA Update*, Issue 3, 1998; italics added).

Third, the differences between U.S. states' income and property taxes, and the effect those differences might have on charitable giving, are significant. Among other things, more taxpayers file itemized returns in high–tax states. For a more detailed discussion of comparing levels of charitable giving in the states, the reader should contact the AAFRC Trust for Philanthropy or read *Giving USA Update*, issue 3, 1998, published by the AAFRC Trust for Philanthropy.

REPEAT GRAPHS

Rather than referring the reader back and forth from chapter to chapter and table to table, we have printed a number of our findings twice. Not only does this make the data easier to follow, it makes each individual chapter more comprehensive. Most of the information included in Chapter 8, "Through the Decades," also appears in earlier parts of the *Index*.

SOURCES

In preparing *The Index of Leading Cultural Indicators: American Society at the End of the 20th Century,* I relied on a wide variety of government documents, academic studies, and books and articles by experts in the respective fields. Those who would like more information on the facts and figures used in the *Index* may be interested in the following annual government publications.

U. S. Department of Commerce, Census Bureau, *Statistical Abstract*

U. S. Department of Justice, Federal Bureau of Investigation, *Crime in the United States*

U.S. Department of Justice, Bureau of Justice Statistics, *Bureau of Justice Statistics Sourcebook*

U.S. Department of Education, *Digest of Education Statistics*

Many government publications are available on the Internet as well as in published format. Some of those that I found most useful in compiling these indicators were:

Census Bureau, *www.census.gov*
- Marital Status and Living Arrangements
- Unmarried-Couple Households, by Presence of Children
- Living Arrangements of Children Under 18 Years Old

National Center for Health Statistics, *www.cdc.gov/nchswww/*
  • National Vital Statistics Report (1998 onwards)
  • Monthly Vital Statistics Report (through 1997)
  • Vital Statistics of the United States

National Center for Education Statistics, *www.nces.ed.gov*
  • The Nation's Report Card
  • Education Statistics Quarterly
  • Highlights from TIMSS

National Institute for Drug Abuse, *www.nida.nih.gov*

National Clearinghouse for Alcohol and Drug Information, *www.health.org/pubs/nhsda/index.htm*

The best place to begin looking for government data on the Internet is *www.fedstats.gov*. It provides a search engine and links to various agencies that provide reliable data on the Web.

In addition, there are a variety of nongovernmental sources that were used. Many of these are available on the Internet.

Alan Guttmacher Institute
120 Wall Street
New York, NY 10005
www.agi-usa.org

Annie E. Casey Foundation
701 St. Paul Street
Baltimore, MD 21202
www.aecf.org

Child Trends
4301 Connecticut Avenue, NW
Washington, DC 20008
www.childtrends.org

Giving USA
AAFRC Trust for Philanthropy
PO Box 1020
Sewickley, PA 15143
www.aafrc.org

Monitoring the Future
Institute for Social Research
University of Michigan
426 Thompson Street
Ann Arbor, MI 48104
www.isr.umich.edu/src/mtf/index2.html

National Center for Policy Analysis
12655 N. Central Expressway
Suite 720
Dallas, TX 75243
www.ncpa.org

National Fatherhood Initiative
One Bank Street
Suite 160
Gaithersburg, MD 20878
www.fatherhood.org

The World Almanac and Book of Facts 1999, edited by Robert
Farnighetti. Mahwah, NJ: Primedia Reference, 1999.